Powering Up

Are Computer Games Changing Our Lives?

Rebecca Mileham

WILEY

dana centre

eat, drink, talk science

Other Wiley Editorial Offices

John Wiley & Sons Inc., 111 River Street, Hoboken, NJ 07030, USA

Jossey-Bass, 989 Market Street, San Francisco, CA 94103-1741, USA

Wiley-VCH Verlag GmbH, Boschstr. 12, D-69469 Weinheim, Germany

John Wiley & Sons Australia Ltd, 42 McDougall Street, Milton, Queensland 4064, Australia

John Wiley & Sons (Asia) Pte Ltd, 2 Clementi Loop #02-01, Jin Xing Distripark, Singapore 129809

John Wiley & Sons Ltd, 6045 Freemont Blvd, Mississauga, Ontario L5R 4J3, Canada

Wiley also publishes its books in a variety of electronic formats. Some content that appears in print may not
be available in electronic books.

British Library Cataloguing in Publication Data
A catalogue record for this book is available from the British Library

ISBN: 978-0-470-72310-4
Typeset in 9.5 on 14 pt SM DIN by SNP Best-set Typesetter Ltd., Hong Kong
Printed and bound by Printer Trento in Italy

Contents

Introduction

In five decades, games have gone from nerds' niche to a cultural phenomenon and multi-million pound, global industry. On the way, they've gathered associations that mean we regard them today with a curious mix of wonder and mistrust.

But I believe they've got a huge amount to offer us all. In this book you can explore the latest scientific research into how games are changing our lives. What's their impact on our **health**? Are games changing the way we **think**? How are our **identities** changing as a result of games, both online and off-line? What is science's view on whether we get **addicted** to games, and if they can make us **violent**? How are games changing the way we **learn**? What's their potential effect on what we **believe**? Finally, what can we say about how they might change – and change us, in the **future**?

By examining what the science is showing, and what the experts are saying, I want to look beyond the fear and the hype and see where computer games could take us next. For the first time, this book brings together the thinkers and doers in computer games research – and tells some stories about the power that computer games really have.

Some of the questions I seek to answer in the book – particularly those connected with the negative impact of games – are those the media ask, and those we ask ourselves as gamers, partners, friends and parents. You'll find plenty of evidence in the book about the bad as well as the good of gaming. But as a result of exploring the answers to these negative questions, I've become convinced that the *other* questions are actually the more important ones.

Rather than asking repeatedly what effects computer games are having on teen-agers' propensity for violence, I wonder if we should be exploring how games can help beat bullying and empower the young? Instead of endless concern about the neurological effects of 'game addiction', why don't we try to take advantage of the idea that our brains find games a wonderful way to learn? And rather than thinking games are childish and trivial because of a few juvenile blockbusters, why can't we focus on the creative and thoughtful games that do exist and say 'This is what we want to play!'?

Who am I to make these claims for games? I don't think I've got the credentials to be considered a gamer, although I've always been surrounded by people who love games.

One of the first computer games I played was called House. It was programmed in the arcane language Fortran by my enterprising dad at his office, on a Rainbow officially intended for performing engineering calculations. My younger brother, Greg, and I would explore its sprawling map, going from room to room in search of treasure – including the fabled jewelled jaglock – while attempting to avoid the Kraak, whose menacing presence was ever-near. If you found the silver sword, you could cut yourself free when goblins tied you up. If you found the emerald earrings, I'm not quite sure what benefit you gained.

At home, I played the platform adventure game Starquake on an Amstrad CPC, and the names of the teleport stations – Vorex, Snody, Quore, the elusive Raliq – still make me go all glassy-eyed. It wasn't a taxing game – indeed, I didn't have any interest in anything more physically or cerebrally challenging. I just enjoyed getting the unstable planet's core elements safely back in order – a job well done. But piano practice took me away from the screen and I don't think I played another game until college.

Greg, on the other hand, put in the required number of hours to be considered a bona fide gamer during his school years. He incidentally picked up a facility with design and programming that form the basis of his professional life today.

I spent my college days in the company of science and engineering students, 80% of whom were male and liked nothing more than a 3-hour bout of frantic 3-D shooter Descent or the spooky adventure game Alone in the Dark. What held much greater attraction for me was the dawn of the first web-browser, Mosaic, and my first, guiltily addictive, sessions on Internet Relay Chat. Exploration, interactivity and conversation – these were activities that pushed my buttons. It made sense that the stunning and immersive Myst should catch my attention, and that the hours I spent playing it should have been in the company of the man I then married.

Yinch is a computer games programmer, and worked crazy hours in the industry while I worked sometimes-crazy hours in my job at the Science Museum, London, and as a science journalist. It didn't leave much time over for gaming. Once we had added two children to our household, the only computer games played tended to be the sort that are brought to you by the letter 'a'. Until we got a Wii, anyway.

I want to change all that now. I've got excited again about playing games as I've researched and written this book. I do want to get back and finish the Myst series – and there are loads more I've got to try. I've also surprised myself by wanting now to *make* games, as some of the people I've talked to do every day. With Yinch in the house, this ought to be feasible – although now that my project is drawing to a close, I ought to let him do some of his own work for a while.

I also want to see what's coming next from the creative people who I've met in the industry – many, many of them fascinating women and men with scientific and gaming credentials galore, and enthusiasm to match. I interviewed 60 experts for the book, picking their considerable brains on topics from psychology to neuroscience, from game design to education, from gaming and its impacts to the technologies of the future. Their knowledge and ideas, so freely shared, I have gratefully received and I hope faithfully represented.

In addition to the interviews, over 150 people contributed their experiences to the book through an online survey. I heard stories from gamers in America, Australia, across Europe and Asia (and one lone entrant from Africa), which have influenced my thinking and colourfully illustrated the book. I hope the sample, not intended to be representative or statistical, gives a flavour of how players really feel about the games they play. A heart-felt thank you to those who revealed their inner gamer.

Inevitably I have made some decisions in how to define and organise the information in the book, which I will briefly explain: I have called all games mediated by computer technology *computer games* whether they're played on a console, a PC, a mobile phone or in virtual reality. I have probably erred on the side of generosity in what I've classified as a game: where games technology – like a Quake engine, for example – is used to explore a scientific principle, that seems valid and revealing. Games might be psychological, exploratory, carried out using VR or a hand-held gadget. The exception is online gambling which has its own literature and is not covered in this book. I do include the online worlds like There and Second Life, which the research shows at least *some* players consider to be games. I see them as arenas in which you see psychological games played all the time; and where it's perfectly possible to experience social death. Sounds like a game to me.

I have received colossal support from Yinch and from my parents in writing the book. Their encouragement, active help and expertise and ingenious entertainment of the children is how I got the project finished. Now that it's done, I do plan to spend more time with my family. Maybe we'll play some computer games.

Glossary

Although it's not necessary to know a lot about computer games to follow the arguments in this book, here are brief definitions of some game terminology I've used:

3-D game – simply, a game that takes place in a world that can be explored in three dimensions rather than two. 2-D games are viewed either as 'top down' (bird's-eye) view or via action that scrolls from screen to screen (see platform game). Early 3-D games often appeared in isometric projection, a simplified way of showing a 3-D environment on a screen. Greater computing power now allows games to process and display 3-D scenes in real time.

Adventure game – these games often involve exploring a world, solving puzzles and looking for clues to work out the solution to a mystery.

Arcade game – games originally played on coin-operated arcade machines, but often now available for the PC, characterised by simple controls and short levels that rapidly increase in difficulty.

Console game – as opposed to a PC (personal computer) game, a console game is played on a dedicated piece of game hardware with a controller, and often displayed on a television.

Engine (as in 'Quake engine') – the underlying core software of a computer game. Engines can often be reused for different games or to allow users to create their own versions of a game.

First-person shooter – players 'see' the world directly through the eyes of their character and progress or achieve goals in the game through the medium of blasting away at enemies using a gun or similar weapon.

Levels – these are the stages of a game, sometimes taking place in a sequence of increasingly challenging environments or against different opponents, through which the player works in order to achieve the outcomes of a level-based game.

PC game – a game available to play on a personal computer (contrast with *arcade game* and *console game*).

Platform game – a type of 2-D game in which players jump to and from platforms or over obstacles as the game scrolls from screen to screen.

Real time – games wherein the action takes place continuously, as opposed to a turn-based game.

Role-playing game – players take on a fictional role, and usually develop the character through a mechanism that reflects experience (for example, work or combat). Massively multiplayer online role-playing games (MMORPGs) can involve thousands of players interacting in a shared environment. Action takes place in a persistent 'world' that develops and changes even when the player is absent, often with a fantasy theme.

Strategy game – a game that requires the player to make plans and high-level decisions to determine the game's outcome (rather than luck or quick reflexes playing a large part).

Turn-based – games in which players take their turn in their own time, instead of all interacting together in real time.

1 Can Computer Games Affect Your Health?

Introduction

Two teenage boys steps onto patterned mats on the floor of their classroom. Their attention is firmly focused on a TV screen in front of them, and they seem oblivious to their peers who crowd around them. A beat starts, then catchy music, and as arrows scroll up the screen, their feet hit corresponding arrows on the mat below. Forwards, backwards, side-to-side, they jump and swivel to keep in time. They're not mucking about or playing for laughs – this is serious dancing. A few minutes later, the manic music and funky footwork are over, and one boy mops his face with his vest.

If you'd told me you could get teenage boys to dance at school, I'd have been sceptical. If you'd told me you could get teenage boys to dance, in their classroom, in broad daylight, in front of a judgemental gaggle of their peers, until they dripped with sweat, I'd have been downright disbelieving. Yet this is what's happening in schools all over the USA. Dance Dance Revolution (DDR) is a computer game based on dancing to music videos created by the Japanese company Konami. The way to play is to follow the arrows that scroll up the screen overlaid on the video: sometimes tapping with a toe, sometimes jumping to place both feet on two arrows at once. The music sets the beat – sometimes steady and reminiscent of aerobics classes, more often frenetic and driving. The more arrows you hit at the right time, the higher your score.

One PE **teacher** has estimated that in a **45-minute class**, **children's steps add** up to running a **mile** and a half

Games like Dance Dance Revolution are motivating schoolchildren to get moving.

The idea to try using gaming equipment in school PE lessons came from an academic at West Virginia University's Motor Development Center. Linda Carson was surprised one day to see a queue of kids waiting to use the arcade version of DDR in a Philadelphia mall. 'There were all these kids dancing and sweating and actually standing in line and paying money to be physically active', she told the *New York Times*. 'And they were drinking water, not soda.'

A trial project in 20 schools was a hit with classes – and now the state plans to install the game in all 765 of its public schools during 2008. One PE teacher has estimated that in a 45-minute class, children's steps add up to running a mile and a half – some even further.

In this chapter, I examine the evidence that computer games can affect your health – for better and worse. Are we breeding an obese generation of computer gamers who can't get off the sofa? Or can all games actually help you keep fit? Do games give you square eyes, or actually improve your vision? And which games have the power to control pain and illness?

Does Gaming Make You Fat?

The Dance Dance Revolution experience really is revolutionary. The idea that a computer game could raise your heart rate and shift some calories is in profound contrast with our cultural perception that games create couch potatoes. In the current climate of concern about obesity, particularly in childhood, screen-based entertainment is usually one of the activities first in the firing line. Indeed, the National Obesity Forum, while acknowledging that the development of child obesity in the UK has not been well researched, lists 'time spent in inactive pursuits' among the potential risks. Its president told the BBC recently that parents 'must stop' their children from 'watching TV and playing computer games all the time – these lifestyle factors are key'.

Parents are understandably concerned about a link between games and muscle-rot. One mother of two young children told me by email: 'In a society where an increasing number of our children are obese, and through the increase in technology have lost their ability to socialize and interact with each other – shouldn't we be advocating physical activity, imaginary play and socializing with real human beings?'

These sound like common-sense concerns. Yet, according to a vocal minority of experts, the received wisdom has no basis in science at all. Michael Gard lectures

Shouldn't children just get outside more to combat the rise of obesity?

in physical education at Charles Sturt University in New South Wales, Australia, where concerns about obesity, TV and gaming are prevalent. He recently completed a 4-year study of assumptions about the causes of obesity, and he's made some rather surprising discoveries. One of the biggest is the realisation that the evidence for a causal link between media use and obesity is extremely scarce: the first simply isn't proven to cause the second.

Michael doesn't deny that obesity is now widespread. In Western countries, up to 70% of adults are now overweight or obese, while up to 40% of children fall into these categories. And it's not that overweight people don't watch TV: 'The research on computers and television suggests that children who use a lot of TV *are* more likely to be heavier and less fit', he told me. But what Michael disputes is the idea that gaming and television *cause* that obesity. He thinks that, as a society, we've got that quite wrong.

Reviews of the research in this **area** say that **many of the children** who do the **most computer game-playing** also do the **most** physical **exercise**

'For years, people were determined to prove a link between obesity and sedentary activities', he tells me. 'There is a common-sense argument that television and games displace physical activity – a rationality that more of one equals less of the other.' The trouble was, no matter how many studies scientists did, the evidence for a link didn't come. In fact, it was rather the opposite.

'There is a consistent finding that TV and computer use is not a very strong predictor of physical activity levels', says Michael. But hang on, aren't we always being told that children who play games are sofa-sluggards? Well, there's more:

'Reviews of the research in this area say that many of the children who do the most computer game-playing also do the most physical exercise.'

Mind-Changing Science

Revolutionary, isn't it? Michael certainly found some resistance in the scientific community to his ideas. 'When I wrote a discussion paper for a British think tank (*Obesity and Public Policy: Thinking clearly and treading carefully*, 2007), a couple of obesity scientists said they had not heard of me; they doubted that I was an academic. They questioned whether I worked for a real university or whether it was a front for the fast food companies.'

This is ironic when you ask Michael what he thinks are the real causes of obesity. 'I feel the problem is the ubiquity of bad quality food. Obesity was flat-lining until 1970, when it spiked up, at the same time as the rise of mega food corporations, and high-calorie food.' Is there scientific evidence that Western tendencies to be 'fast food nations' is to blame? Michael admits the published evidence is still patchy. 'Most research that tries to track people's average caloric intake since the early twentieth century doesn't find any change. But there's been a huge increase in production of chocolate and soft drinks, even though people don't report eating more food. Well, those snacks have got to be going somewhere.' He suspects that people have stopped classifying snacking as eating. 'The fast food companies' strategy is to make it normal to eat between meals', he explains.

Despite these findings, the 'unhealthy gaming' myth has yet to be busted in popular culture. Renowned children's author Michael Morpurgo contributed a telling foreword to a book published in 2007 entitled *How to stop your kids watching too much TV, spending hours on the computer, wasting days on the GameBoy, endlessly texting friends, etc . . .* He wrote:

'Now children have in-house entertainment of every conceivable variety, and all instantly available, instantly stimulating. Like fast food, it is seductive and compelling, and can become deeply habit-forming. Like fast food, too much of it is seriously bad for you. We know that.'

But it turns out we don't know that at all. To Michael Gard, there are strongly social reasons for views such as this. 'There is a long-standing suspicion of technology that is quite deep-rooted in our culture', he says. 'There was even an argument in the scientific literature for a while that TVs and games were *more* sedentary than other sedentary pursuits, like reading – they were supposed to be putting children into a zombie-like state. There was never much evidence.'

Nonetheless, the link goes on being made. The British Dietetic Association (BDA) reported in June 2006 that children spend two and a half months on average each

The rise in obesity began with the rise of easily available high-calorie food, according to Michael Gard.

year staring at screens. The survey of 3000 school children found a fifth of their time was spent playing video games, watching TV and using computers. It was a finding worth serious consideration in terms of physical and social impacts. But instead, the BDA used it as hook for obesity warnings and diet advice.

It may not even make sense to put computer games in the same category of activity as watching television and videos. Research published in 2006 questioned whether computer-game playing should be called 'sedentary'. Academics at the Exercise and Sport Science Department of the University of Miami measured the metabolic responses of 21 boys aged 7 to 10 as they played Tekken 3 for 15 minutes on a PlayStation. They found that the boys expended a significant amount of energy playing the game, showing increased respiratory rate and ventilation – the equivalent of walking at 2 miles per hour. OK, so the children didn't exactly get out of breath – it wasn't quite enough for the experience to be rated as 'moderate activity'. But the calories expended would, the researchers calculated, add up to a weight loss of 1.8 kg a year if the player spent an average time at the keyboard or console: hardly a recipe for increasing flab.

It **may not** even **make sense** to put **computer games** in the same **category** of activity as **watching television** and **videos**

Another significant difference between gaming and other activities is that, when your hands are busy with a keyboard or game controller, it's impossible to do much 'junk eating'. Research suggests that one factor in children becoming overweight is the over-consumption of foods deliberately marketed to young people. And there certainly is a lot of food advertising: one American study estimated that during children's television programming, viewers were exposed to one food advertisement every 5 minutes. An influential obesity report (*The Role of Media in Childhood Obesity*, Kaiser Family Foundation 2004) noted that 'From SpongeBob Cheez-Its to Hulk pizzas and Scooby-Doo Marshmallow cereals, today's grocery aisles are filled with scores of products using kids' favorite characters to sell them food.'

Some academics are now joining Gard in his unconventional views. And if the science doesn't support claims that screens equal obesity, maybe health professionals need collectively to rethink their public pronouncements, says Michael Gard. 'If experts want to advise parents about how they should parent – or to advise any of us about how we should live – then it is probably a good idea to base this advice on sound assumptions'.

Could Gaming Make You Fit?

Gaming doesn't make you fat. So could it help you stay fit – or get fitter? If Dance Dance Revolution isn't your game, there are other bits of kit that might be. Research published in January 2007 showed that playing a computer game that required players to move about – unsurprisingly – used more energy than a sedentary one. The project indicated that by playing a game that used a controller such as a Nintendo Wii, players could triple energy expenditure.

It's not the only get-up-and-play technology available. Research at Heriot-Watt University examined how much physical exertion was involved in playing games using Sony PlayStation's EyeToy. 'I tried an EyeToy by chance, and I found myself quite breathless after only a couple of minutes playing one of the games', says Alasdair Thin, a lecturer in human physiology. 'So I figured that active gaming may well have the potential to be a novel form of exercise.'

The Kinetic Videogame is designed as a workout, with a virtual personal trainer and exercise schedules. 'We decided to independently test it against a standard exercise test on a cycle ergometer', explains Alasdair. 'It was possible that the game might be either too easy or too hard and therefore limit the intensity of exercise that the subjects could engage in.'

During testing, young adult players waved their arms, kicked or nodded their heads while having their heart rate and oxygen consumption measured. The 10-minute aerobic session of the game Cascade resulted in the subjects' heart rates reaching the lower end of the range recommended by the experts (the American College of Sports Medicine) for a training effect. Intense 3-minute bouts of Sidewinder raised the players' heart rates to the top end of this range. After a total of 36 minutes' playing time, Thin calculated that each player had expended on average about 300 calories – about the amount you'd use walking briskly for an hour. 'Not only does it provide a fun way to exercise and if you want, even a degree of competition with others', said Alasdair, 'It also may help individuals who want to exercise in private if, for instance, they lack confidence, have poor coordination or body image issues.'

So it's good news for all of us who prefer to wear Lycra behind firmly closed doors. And researchers are looking creatively at new ways to use the power of gaming to keep us on the move. Educational innovator Futurelab, based in Bristol, UK, has devised a wrist-mounted pet aimed at getting children to exercise more. The tamagotchi-style creature, known as a Fizzee, measures the wearer's heart-rate and motion, using a scoring system to relate the figures to the health of the digital pet.

Dan Sutch, the Futurelab researcher who initiated the project, told me how Fizzees were intended to promote health: 'Obesity isn't only caused by children not getting enough exercise – the problem includes diet, economic and social issues, education and understanding too. Fizzees tackle two of these elements – exercise and education.' The game element of the Fizzee was key in creating an engaging activity: 'We wanted to develop an approach that children would choose to become involved in and could become immersed in, as they do with digital pets and games', says Dan.

Fizzees are a pet, a game and a learning device rolled into one – and the user chooses which way to engage. 'You can be a player, earning points and overcoming challenges. You can learn, investigating ways to stay healthy and putting it into practice. And you can also be a carer, nurturing the digital pet by keeping active', Dan explained.

How have children responded? In the small-scale study so far, the feedback's been really good. 'Fizzee appealed to all the children, but in different ways', Dan told me. 'One girl, for example took on the role of nurturing the Fizzee and did activities that were best for the Fizzee. Another boy saw the Fizzee as "someone else in the gym" to exercise alongside.'

Futurelab is hoping to start a craze: the technology also allows children to collaborate via a Fizzee website, comparing their pets, swapping activities and looking at their past fitness records. They've already observed children comparing each other's on-screen progress by holding the screens next to each other.

In another ploy to keep kids moving, Gymkids have launched exercise equipment for primary school children that links to any game on any Sony PlayStation. If you don't keep stepping on the Step2Play, the game abruptly ceases. Alternatively, the Cyberbike comes with five games that link to the television. Keep cycling or it all stops working.

And GameCycle is an upper-body exercise system suitable for wheelchair users, which combines arm cranking (moving handles up and down simultaneously) with Nintendo GameCube racing games. Studies showed that working with the

Fizzees: a pet, a game and a learning device rolled into one.

The wrist-mounted Fizzee measures the wearer's heart rate and motion and relates it to the health of a digital pet.

COURTESY OF FUTURELAB, FIZZEES 2007

GameCycle resulted in more calories being burnt – even though players didn't perceive they'd worked harder. Research published in 2006 on teenagers with mobility impairments due to spina bifida, showed that 87% increased their maximum exercise capability after training with the GameCycle.

Studies showed that **working** with the *GameCycle* **resulted** in **more calories being burnt – even though** players **didn't perceive** they'd **worked harder**

Cyberbikes help keep primary school children fit. Keep cycling to keep playing the game.

The GameCycle links to a Nintendo GameCube.

Players burn more calovies with the Game Cycle, even though they don't notice they're doing it.

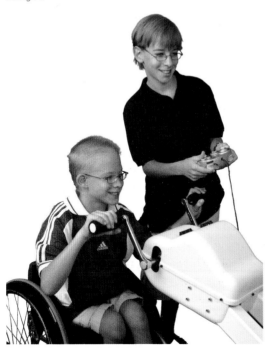

In step with the schools in West Virginia who've benefited from Dance Dance Revolution, Groby Community College in Leicestershire has been using dance mats to promote exercise among girls. When the sports hall was in use for exams, and the 16-year-old girls didn't want to go outside, head of PE, Martyn Thompson saw dance mats as a way to get them moving. And it did. 'All of a sudden they had something in sport that they were good at', Martyn told me. 'It was recognition – good for their self-esteem. And they were the experts. Ultimately they knew more about this than me.' Even habitual non-attenders started appearing for energetic dance sessions.

Martyn extended the lesson by getting the girls to plan their own routines, which they practised away from the dance mats. He's working on ways to incorporate learning about muscle groups, bones and the benefits of exercise 'without the baggage of PE'. And he's noticed several advantages over traditional sports lessons: increased self-motivation to improve, better social interaction in lessons and an interest in getting fitter. It sounds as though 'games' may finally have come of age.

Sorry Boss, I've Got a (Virtual) Sports Injury

Like all forms of exercise, digital workouts come with a warning. As soon as Nintendo's Wii reached people's living rooms, news reports emerged about its capacity to inflict injury on those using it – or those standing innocently nearby. Gamers told of tennis serves attempted underneath low light fittings; shoulder strain caused by over-enthusiastic tenpin bowling and controllers flying out of gamers' hands (towards heads/vases/televisions) with predictable results. Nintendo soon issued a stronger safety strap to avoid the latter accident. In my own household, disaster has only narrowly been averted several times. The 2-year-old member of the family insists on running forward to see whether the bowling ball is going to hit the pins – while the dedicated bowler is still authentically swinging their arm.

It's not the first time gaming products have caused problems through sheer popularity and players' enthusiasm. Nintendonitis (or PlayStation Thumb) was widely reported as new consoles swept the culture. Otherwise known as gamer's grip, it is a condition similar to repetitive strain injury, causing swelling and pain in the finger or thumb joints. In serious cases, the condition may lead to tennis elbow and carpal tunnel syndrome.

'I've got tendonitis in my shoulder, and in one of the Wii games you have to hit 30 baseballs 125 metres', Michelle told me. 'You really swing, and it's aaarghhhh!' Kar On from Singapore said 'Wii Sports provides almost real-life sporting experience in your living room. But I have hurt my back while bowling without proper warming up and stretching.' I ought to mention that Kar On is my father-in-law, and at 67 is a dedicated Wii-bowler and golfer.

David, 38, told me in answer to the question 'What do you like most about Wii Sports?' that he enjoyed 'nearly decapitating my nephew.' In explanation he said that he had successfully beaten his mother at the game by realising that she would not want to cause the passing toddlers any harm, thus handing him a tactical advantage.

Alasdair Thin at Heriot-Watt University has also heard of a few problems: 'There have been some reports of overuse injuries with the Nintendo Wii which focuses more on shoulder and arm movement. The EyeToy games that I have seen tend to involve more body movement and therefore place less strain on individual joints. It's important that games include some form of warm-up activity and provide a way for players to build up their skill and fitness over a period of time.' Alasdair added: 'It's my great hope that appropriately designed "active games" can act as a stepping stone for people to become regularly physically active.'

Can Games Tackle Physical Problems?

Games' potential to help people recover from physical and psychological injury (not just those inflicted by games themselves) has been under test in a number of labs, hospitals and companies. Back in 1988, a study with upper-limb burn victims found good rehabilitation results using computer games controlled by a range of large and small joysticks. Therapists found that games helped their patients overcome fears, as well as distracting them from pain. Far from being sterile or artificial, players found the computer-based therapy encouraged natural hand and arm movements by providing feedback.

And the power of game-based therapy to motivate people undergoing therapy has been underlined continuously since then. In 1993, scientists were already working with 20 people experiencing spasticity in their arm as a result of brain injury. The results showed that the game generated a much wider range of motion than a rote exercise. Indeed, many participants carried on playing their 'therapy' even when they'd completed the session. What's not to like?

Life-Changing Play

GestureTek is a California-based company with an intriguing story. It pioneered the use of camera-enabled computer control – the art of telling a computer what to do simply by moving your body. Today, GestureTek technology is used in countless locations from hospitals to top corporate offices, for therapy, for video-conferencing and in toys (it's licensed to Sony for the EyeToy). But it started out with very different uses, as its creator Vincent John Vincent explained.

'Back in 1986 when Francis MacDougall and I first created this technology, I had just graduated with a psychology degree and was working as a psychotherapist', Vincent told me. 'The technology got people excited about engaging their full body

Saving a goal, avoiding a shark, playing the drums or beating an opponent at volleyball: these games make physical therapy fun. Stroke patients who played Sharkbait reported enhanced balance and movement skills.

REPRINTED WITH PERMISSION FROM GESTURETEK HEALTH™

in virtual activities, and so part of our intention was to use it as a tool in psycho-therapy and rehabilitation. However, most of the early applications were in the area of live stage performance, educational and experiential museum and science center installations, as well as a TV production tool.'

The stage performances to which Vincent refers were something really new. His idea was to reverse the role of the dancer, from one of dancing *to* the music, to creating music and visual effects directly from the performer's movements. He worked with MacDougall to make the Mandala Virtual Reality System which allowed Vincent to use his skills in dance, music and juggling to create unique stage shows.

'In 1995, a therapist purchased a system to use in clinical work, and to do research', says Vincent. 'The results were positive right from the start, with patients consistently doing their therapy for two to three times longer, and being two to three times more eager to participate in sessions. There are now over 200 systems in therapeutic use around the world.'

Ron Kelusky now leads GestureTek's health division, working with a version of the technology called IREX. He explains why the system is so suited for rehabilitation. 'We've found that people have a tendency to want to engage with virtual reality games even if they aren't usually motivated by conventional exercise, or tend to lose interest over time. It's a mixture of cognitive and physical stimulation, which can lead to a reduction in the amount of support people need to live their life.'

In a typical game, the system projects a player's image onto a computer screen, where they can interact with a virtual game or activity that automatically adjusts to their capability – and stretches it, bit by bit.

'Our technology is unencumbered: there's no remote device, no wires, you don't need to have tracking dots stuck on you. You're immersed in a graphical experience so that you can react in real time. It's also realistic – if I move my arm 90 degrees from my hip, that's what I see on the screen', Ron told me. That's of great importance when the change from lifting your arm 10 degrees to 20 degrees might be an incredible physical achievement.

In one notable experiment, patients who'd had a stroke more than a year previously – and thus tended to be resistant to further therapy – tried playing games using IREX. To enhance players' motion, balance, stepping and walking skills, scientists asked them to play virtual games involving swimming with sharks, or snowboarding down a narrow slope.

The experiments were intensive. The patients, who had experienced paralysis on one side of their body as a result of a stroke, played the games for an hour a day over a 4-week period. Players of the snowboarding game had to leap out of the way of obstacles while those in the swimming game bobbed up and down to avoid being virtually eaten. After the therapy, the majority of players reported in the post-test questionnaire that their use of the weaker limb was improved. Daily activities such as getting in and out of the bath, stepping onto the kerb or even putting on trousers were now possible for them.

Brain imaging after the experiment showed the root of the improvement. 'The games seem to create some cortical redevelopment', says Kelusky, 'and they've now found the same in people with cerebral palsy. The more that people manage to do reaching and flexing exercises, the less need there is for surgical intervention or medication.'

Can Gaming Cure a Stressed-Out Mind?

What use might games be in a different sort of therapy – the kind practised on your mind? Scientists and psychologists are now using the latest game technology and or psychological techniques to treat mental and psychiatric disorders.

'It's pretty real. The vibration and the sights and sounds and everything were pretty darn close. I was waiting for shrapnel overhead', Eugene Gochicoa told the *Los Angeles Times* in 2007. Gochicoa, a Navy corpsman 1st class, was describing a game-based simulation called Virtual Iraq. 'It did kind of take me back to when I was back there . . . except I knew I was safe here.'

Gochicoa is an army medic who served in Iraq and came back unscathed. But research shows that up to 15% of personnel returning from Iraq suffer post-traumatic stress disorder (PTSD). Universities, companies and the US government are now spending millions of dollars on recreating the traumatic scenes of the battlefield in a game environment based on modern US-Army soldier simulation Full Spectrum Warrior. Their aim is to immerse veterans in the sights and sounds of combat in order to help them overcome debilitating memories of their experiences.

Once PSTD-sufferers have begun treatment for their fears, Virtual Iraq can be used to heighten the intensity of their recollections. Patients wear a helmet and goggles, and mount a vibrating platform that simulates movement. A joystick allows them to travel through the scene at their own speed. Biofeedback systems monitor respiration, heart rate and palm sweat as the therapist controls events such as explosions, gunfire, fog and even the smells that accompany a scene. Patient and psychologist talk throughout the experience about feeling and responses to what's unfolding.

It's early days in the programme, but results are looking promising. In part-icular, army chiefs hope that the system might be more acceptable than traditional therapy to the generation that's grown up playing war simulation games.

From the hell of war to the grimness of road accidents: for up to 38% of people treated in hospital after a car crash, getting back behind the wheel is a real challenge. To investigate ways of tackling this 'accident phobia', scientists in Ireland, Korea and California collaborated on an approach using computer games. They asked 14 sufferers to try driving in a virtual environment, and also playing city-based driving games including London Racer and the more realistic Midtown Madness. Of the group, half found the experience so immersive that they started to get anxious – their hearts beating faster, and their distress increasing. This was just what the researchers were hoping for, as it provided a safe situation in which to undertake cognitive therapy to combat their fears. The team reported that their findings 'suggest that . . . game reality may have a useful role in the treatment of driving phobia post-accident event when co-morbid conditions such as post-traumatic stress disorder and depression are present.'

What about if your phobia is seemingly less serious – but still causes you stress? Arachnophobia is another candidate for treatment using games. A team at the Cyberpsychology Lab at the University of Quebec used the game editor of seminal 3-D first-person adventure game Half Life so that it contained unnatural numbers of spiders – from small stationary creatures (level one) to scurrying spiders the size of dogs (level three, and stop that screaming). Patients wore head-mounted virtual reality goggles to experience this world of worry, turning their heads to shift their virtual viewpoint. And the results were surprisingly good. After 12 sessions, 24 of the 30 arachnophobes in the study could stand next to a tarantula in an open terrarium. Stephane Bouchard explains 'What we've just shown is that the emotional part of the brain is processing the experience as if it were real.'

A game based on psychology research is one way to cope if your parents are divorcing, according to a company based in Tel Aviv. Zipland Interactive released a game Earthquake in Zipland in 2007, designed to help children aged 9–12 deal with the emotional issues involved when parents separate. The game begins in Zipland, a small paradise island comprising two parts held together by a zip, which represents the marriage of the parents (the King and Queen). When an earthquake rips the island into two, leaving the king and the queen on separate islands, the hero Moose sets out on a quest to reunite the two islands. He initially wants to fix things so that life can go on as before – but learns as part of his adventure that it isn't his responsibility – or indeed a realistic mission.

Critics feel that Earthquake in Zipland may lack the latest gameplay and graphics, but in terms of subject area, the game seems to be innovative. Chaya Harash is a Family Therapist and CEO of Zipland Interactive, with 25 years of experience dealing with family, children, couples and divorce therapy. 'Everyone knows that divorce has a terrible impact on the children involved. Now, parents and psychologists have a tool that can actually interact with a child whose parents are separated or divorced, in order to help him handle the drastic changes in his or her life', she said.

Games to Raise Your Self-Esteem

Need a boost that's something more than coffee first thing in the morning? Games to increase your self-esteem are showing great promise at McGill University, Montreal, Canada. Dr Mark Baldwin and his team are investigating whether games could tackle anxiety and insecurity – an often-unconscious feeling of expectation that people will reject you.

In one game, Eye Spy, players are asked to pick the one smiling face out of a grid of 16. By getting people with low self-esteem to do this task repeatedly and as fast as possible, tests showed they became better at ignoring rejection and seeking the positive. Another game, Wham!, used conditioning to make mental links between the player's name, birthdate and smiling, approving faces. Grow Your Own Chi is a third game that combines some of the results of the first two games with more engaging gameplay.

'These basic principles could be implemented in almost any kind of game. The important thing is to build expectancies of and attention to positive social experiences, rather than focusing on threats, rejections or criticisms', Mark Baldwin told me by email.

What may be really significant is that gameplay of a certain kind is showing ways to reduce aggressive thoughts and feelings often associated with low self-esteem. The latest finding shows a potential way to deal with social rejection – a sense of which can lead to an aggressive response.

'We tested a computer-based intervention designed to boost players' sense of social connection', said Dr Baldwin. Ninety-seven young people aged 9 to 15 first completed a conditioning game on computer which repeatedly paired their own name with images of social acceptance (versus a control condition with no systematic pairing). 'They subsequently reported how aggressive they would feel in response to being rejected by a peer. Those completing the self-acceptance conditioning (particularly those low in self-esteem) reported less aggressive feelings and intentions.'

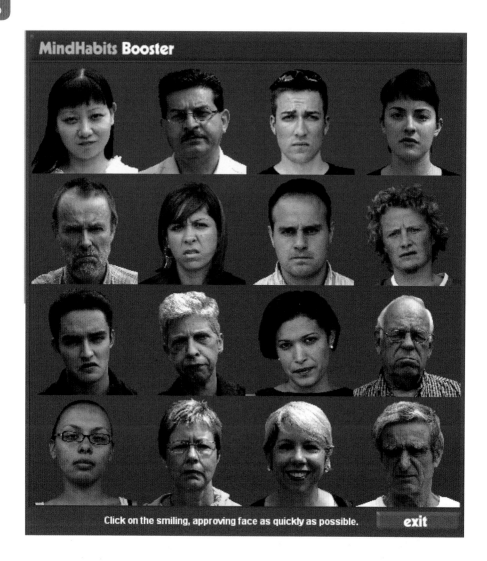

MindHabits **Booster**

Click on the smiling, approving face as quickly as possible. **exit**

Can a game improve your self-esteem? Researchers at McGill University in Montreal use games to combat unconscious expectations of rejection.

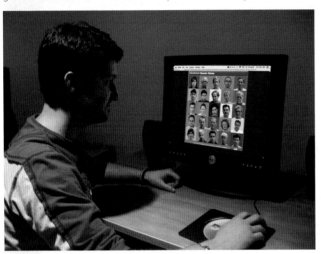

How Can Games Help Treat Brain Disorders?

Epilepsy is one of the most common serious neurological diseases. In 1999, a team at Brandeis University in Massachusetts, USA, created a computer maze game to help shed light on the condition. The maze game first led players through a series of twists and turns, and then asked them to recreate the trip using their memories of the previous route. Each participant, severely epileptic, tried the game while wired up to a bank of instruments measuring their brain's electrical activity. Resulting read-outs showed that, while the gamers were attempting to remember their way through the most difficult parts of the maze, their brains produced theta waves – a type of useful brain wave where groups of neurons fire at the same time. It was the first time that theta waves had been definitely linked to spatial memory in humans, and researchers hoped that the finding would shed light on how this rhythmic activity often goes awry in epileptics' brains.

A few years later in 2003, Brandeis researchers turned to games again as they investigated how humans navigate, by using patients who were already wired up to monitors to investigate their epileptic seizures. Detailed brain activity was visible as players undertook a memory-intensive game in which they explored a virtual town by taxi. The players searched for passengers who appeared in random locations and delivered them to designated stores. The results turned up three kinds of brain cells individually attuned to the tasks of working out where you are, what you see and what you are looking for.

'Our study shows how cells in the human brain rapidly learn to respond to complex features of our environment', said Michael Kahana, associate professor at Brandeis University and an expert in the neurophysiology of human spatial navigation. 'One of the most intriguing discoveries was that some cells respond to combinations of place, view and goal. For example, we found cells that responded to viewing an object only when that object was a goal.'

The team hoped their findings would hold unique information about how human memory works and present new avenues of investigation for treatment of memory disorders such as Alzheimer's disease.

Do Computer Games Give You Square Eyes?

If you were worried about computer games turning your eyes square – or if you've been playing a 3-D game, perhaps that should be cubic – you may have good reason. Research by the Australian National University in Canberra showed there was a reason why 80% of young people were affected by myopia in Singapore, up from only 25% three decades before. Their youthful eyes were responding to many hours spent indoors – some of them inevitably spent looking at electronic screens of various kinds – and had changed shape. The elongated eye was better at focusing short distances, but struggled outdoors.

But there is some good news. In fact, there's evidence that gaming enhances visual skill. Yes, you read that right. Researchers Daphne Bavelier and Shawn Green at the University of Rochester, New York, found back in 2003 that action game players reacted to fast-moving objects more efficiently and could track 30% more objects than non-gamers – skills that are essential for many action-packed tasks.

How did they come to imagine that visual skill might be *improved* by games? Shawn Green explained to me that they'd been planning an experiment to investigate the visual acuity of congenitally deaf people. 'The primary focus of our lab is visual plasticity and how experience shapes the organisation of the visual system', Shawn explained. 'I realized that my own visual skills, along with those of several of my friends, were better than what had been reported in the literature. As at the time I was an avid video game player (as were my friends), so my advisor, Daphne Bavelier, and I decided to test the hypothesis that video game experience was the origin of the observed differences.'

And so it seemed. The researchers asked a group of non-gamers to play the action computer game Medal of Honor for at least 1 hour per day for 2 weeks. As a control, another group played puzzle-oriented game Tetris. After just 2 weeks the group trained on Medal of Honor showed a marked increase in their test performances, whereas the Tetris players did not.

'Action video games require effective monitoring of a large portion of the visual field in order to effectively detect multiple fast-moving peripheral targets', explained Daphne Bavelier. 'Tetris on the other hand requires rather focused attention on the current piece as well as other higher-level processes such as mental rotation.'

Support for the idea that game-players see better came in 2006. A University of Toronto researcher established that computer-game players are also faster at searching out visual information. Alan Castel asked gamers and non-gamers to perform a standard 'crowding' task of spotting an object among a group of other objects on a computer screen, and then quickly pressing a button. Gamers reacted a tenth of a second faster than non-gamers – a significant difference in this domain.

People **who played action games** for a **few hours** each day could **improve** their performance in **eye examinations** by **about 20%**

The gamers used the same searching technique as the non-gamers, but game players were faster and more efficient at carrying out the search. Castel believes computer games help people practise performing searches and the accompanying mental processes, which is why games can be effective in training where visual searching is important.

Back at the University of Rochester, Bavelier and Green showed, in 2007, that people who played action games for a few hours each day could improve their performance in eye examinations by about 20%. To make this claim, the team first had to find candidates for the experiment who had played almost no computer games in the preceding year. On campus, that alone was a challenge.

Once identified as non-gamers, students took a normal eye test (like the ones you see at the optician's) and also a 'crowding' test like the one in Castel's experiment. Then the training began. One group played frenetic team-based shooter Unreal Tournament for 30 hours – over about a 4-week period – while the second group played the more pedestrian Tetris. Afterwards, the group that played Unreal Tournament now scored on average 20% better on the optician's eye test.

There's evidence that these beneficial effects of computer games are long-lasting – a separate experiment that involved two sight tests, found that 10 hours' training was still reaping rewards 5 months later. But it's not totally clear why these effects are taking place. Is it that gaming enhances the brain's sensory process-ing? Do action games result in an increased capacity in the visual short-term memory? Research is continuing in pursuit of the answer.

In one instance at least, a game is having amazing results in treating an eye condition. Normally, sufferers of amblyopia wear a patch to encourage their weaker eye to use its neural connections. It's a condition that affects lots of children, many of whom require 400 hours of patching to gain effective results. But a team at Nottingham University used a racing computer game to show that there may be a short cut. By using a virtual reality headset, they fed images of the player's racing car to the weaker eye, and images of all the rest of the field to the stronger eye, giving a strong incentive for the brain to pay atten-tion to the car the player was trying to control. Astonishingly, scientists saw the effect of 400 hours of patching in only 1 hour. Scientists are now trying to discover why the breakthrough is effective with some children, but not with certain others.

Games to Numb Pain and Deal with Disease

There's quite a lot of evidence that gaming can help cure cancer. It's not a direct effect. But a number of studies have found that chemotherapy is more bearable with a game to play. Distracted patients report less nausea and lower blood pressure after treatment than those with nothing else to think about – and ask for fewer painkillers too.

It's also been found that cancer patients recover more quickly by playing a computer game designed to teach them about the disease. Results from a study conducted in Australia, Canada and the USA show that a specially designed game called Re-Mission has beneficial health effects for young cancer patients. During the game, players lead a 'nanobot' character called Roxii as she travels through the bodies of fictional cancer patients, destroying cancer cells, defending against infection and battling the often life-threatening side-effects of cancer and its treatments. As the game says: 'It's the world's smallest battlefield, but the stakes have never been higher.'

Cancer patients **recover more quickly** by playing a **computer** game **designed** to **teach them** about the **disease**

In a choice of 20 missions, players are challenged to calm a stressed girl so that her MRI scan will be effective, encourage patients to take their medication or painkillers, and help a boy to avoid infection. It's all the information you'd probably find in a patient leaflet – and yet presented using great graphics and funky music, and with proper gameplay. Earlier and simpler games such as Packy and Marlon, which helps children cope with diabetes, have also been shown to reduce hospital visits and improved self-care.

Do games have power over pain? It seems they may. Researchers at the Wheeling Jesuit University in West Virginia wanted to test the effects of different genres of computer game – action, puzzle, arcade, fighting, sport and boxing – on their ability to distract players from pain. How could they find out – while remaining on the right side of the ethics committee? Firstly, test subjects had 15 minutes to

Can you help Roxii destroy cancer cells? Young cancer patients who played Re-Mission maintained higher blood levels of chemotherapy, suggesting they were sticking to therapy regimes. They also demonstrated greater knowledge about cancer, self-belief and ability to communicate about the disease compared with a non-playing group.

BRAIN CANCER CELL

bpm 80

PATIENT HISTORY

PATIENT NAME: Taylor DeGrasso

AGE: 17   **GENDER:** Female

DIAGNOSIS: Brain Tumor

Taylor was diagnosed with medulloblastoma, a brain tumor. She presented with severe headaches and dizziness. She had a complete resection of her tumor followed by radiation therapy to the tumor site, full brain and spine over 6 weeks. She is now on weekly chemo maintenance. She requires Magnetic Resonance Imaging (MRI) to make sure there are no tumor cells in her spinal column and is anxious about her upcoming MRI.

LAUNCH   ESC - CANCEL

MISSION BRIEFING

Roxxi, you are to tag along on a spinal tap to seek out and destroy any brain tumor cells that might have entered the spinal column. If you spot any, destroy them quickly, as they become harder to kill once they are latched on. Be warned, fear of the spinal tap has made Taylor very stressed. Electrical nerve flares may cause you to short-circuit unless you calm her with some deep breathing exercises.

LAUNCH

ESC - CANCEL

practise and play each game. Then, they each agreed to dip one foot into a tub of icy water, and try to play for another 5 minutes. All of those playing games managed to play for longer than a control group with no game to distract from their discomfort. But those given sports or fighting games were able to withstand more pain than those playing any other genre. With more sensory overload from the game, the pain had less chance of making itself felt.

The discovery raises the prospect that trips to the dentist or painful injections could be made easier by providing patients with the right kind of computer game to distract them.

The potential for games to distract patients from pain was recognised back in 1987. By filling up someone's cognitive field with tasks that consume attention, games helped to focus a person's mind away from pain.

Out of 150 respondents to my gamer survey, only one talked about a serious health condition with a potential games link. Chris, 29, told me 'I suffered a pulmonary embolism (PE) last year, which I can't fully attribute to online gaming, but it may have contributed. I had a leg injury which meant I was off work, so being the World of Warcraft (WoW) addict I was, I turned to the game and played from the moment I woke up until last thing at night. Fortunately I am now fully recovered, both from the PE and WoW, but it's made me realise the dangers of sitting at a PC for a long time, particularly if you use a PC at work and at home too.'

I suffered a **pulmonary embolism** last year, which **I can't** fully attribute to **online gaming**, but **it may have contributed**

Other gamers reported a few very mild physical issues. Quite a few mentioned 'getting less sleep' including a Metal Gear Solid player aged 37 and Rachid, 28, who plays 3-D platform shooter Metroid Prime 3. Becks, 27, told of 'perspiration and a bit of pushing and shoving' during EyeToy games, while another gamer, aged 29, reported a severe case of 'pointerfinger due to the endless slashing of ghouls' in fantasy action role-playing game Diablo II. Angela, 62, said that playing Bubbles had made her hands hurt – it's more dangerous than it looks. Even the light-hearted action game Lego Star Wars II took its toll: Henry, 39, found it had caused a bit of eye strain and neck ache.

More apparent were the benefits people found in game playing during illness or tough times. 'I have met a great number of new people I count as friends, both online and in real life', reported one 41-year-old There player. 'It has been very helpful when I was ill and could not interact in the real world for a period of time.' Chad, 19, said of Mafia 'I think it's gotten me some rough times in my life. Just having it is a way to escape some daily life issues.'

And Nick Yee, a well-known computer games researcher, has further evidence of the power of play. He blogged extensively about an antibiotic reaction he experienced while suffering from a drug-resistant infection. He woke up one day to find his entire upper body was affected by a deep rash that caused terrible itching, accompanying the pain from the underlying illness. 'The medications weren't helping much', he told me. But fortunately he had two new Nintendo DS games: Ouendan 2 and Pokemon Diamond/Pearl. 'In a strange, twisted way, the games helped me make it through the 3–4 days when the allergic reaction peaked. The games were the only thing that could take my mind off the pain and the uncontrollable itching.' One game was rhythm-based, the other gradual and growth-based. By alternating between the two, he turned his mind away from the intense pain and discomfort that he says gave him fleeting thoughts of suicide.

Conclusion

Are games good or bad for your health? Many in the media, ably assisted by branches of the health lobby, would like us to believe that games are a cultural evil contributing to a downward spiral of flab and sloth. But with the evidence we've seen in this chapter, this view seems outdated and ill-informed.

In my research I found the power of games for good everywhere I looked. As well as illustrating how games can keep you fit, the projects in this chapter show that games can tackle ills of body and mind. Some play on games' reward system for exercise, rehabilitation or distraction from pain. Some use novel technologies or software to treat psychological problems. Some reveal the way our bodies work using games – and even make them work more effectively.

With this evidence, it's hard to explain why games still have such negative cultural associations for some people – whether it's the obesity watchdogs or the literary snobs. 'The fact that Harry Potter is celebrated but games are not seems to be entirely cultural', said Michael Gard, the Australian academic who's busted the myth that gaming increases your girth. 'It's inexplicable in scientific terms.'

I've been surprised at the enormous range, diversity and quality of games and game technology at work in health promotion and medical treatment. Many creative researchers are starting to exploit game technology in new ways, and seeing remarkable results. As word spreads about the power of play for health, perhaps many more will follow in their pioneering footsteps – and those who peddle the negative stereotypes will finally have to admit they've been wrong.

2 Can Computer Games Change the Way You Think?

Introduction

On the banks of the timeless Thames in London stands the House of Lords. This suitably ancient-looking building is a symbol of the British establishment: traditional, eminent and dripping in history. And as the upper house of the Parliament of the UK, perhaps the most powerful idea for which it stands is the authority of age.

Here, elder statesmen and women gather to apply their collective wisdom to matters of national importance. In these august surroundings, noble Lords – many of considerable cultural or political distinction – have turned their minds to scrutinising the whippersnapperish lower house, and applying their independent expertise to the order of the day.

Whatever your personal politics, the cultural message is clear: age means maturity and seniority. As I write this, the average age of members of the House of Lords is 68. And it's here in the House of Lords, in an antique wood-panelled room with William Morris wallpaper, that Baroness Susan Greenfield has chosen to launch a rather significant product.

Professor Greenfield is a prominent neuroscientist who was created a life peer in June 2001. She's Director of the Royal Institution of Great Britain, has written several popular books about consciousness, and has 29 honorary degrees. But what she's talking about today speaks not only to her public persona but her private life.

'I want a fulfilling life into old age', she tells a roomful of scientists and journalists. 'I have a 92-year-old father. I'm worried', the 57-year-old said, 'about the time

The House of Lords is a symbol of the British establishment: traditional, eminent and authoritative.

when I'm on my Zimmer-frame, and there are people looking after me.' Today, our most common associations with ideas of ageing are becoming negative. As more of us live much longer in the West, there's enormous cultural concern about our cognitive skills – those faculties that allow us to think and know, to judge, and to be aware we are doing it.

> **❙❙** It's possible **literally** to **lose your mind. We lose** the ability to **evaluate,** and start **seeing things** like **children** again **❙❙**

Greenfield turns our attention to a picture of neurons and their branching connections. 'These stringy bits proliferate as we grow up, our experiences influencing and shaping our brains. This is called plasticity. But as we age, the branches can be pruned back – through senility.' The terror of baby boomers, many of whom have seen their parents experience the devastation that ageing can bring, is confirmed by science. 'It's possible literally to lose your mind. We lose the ability to evaluate, and start seeing things like children again: how sweet, how fast, how bright, how cold.'

There's no magic pill to combat this, says Baroness Greenfield. So, out of a self-professed passion for evidence-based ways of tackling cognitive decline, Greenfield is launching MindFit. This new software provides a personalised programme of computer games that exercise 14 different mental skills. And by playing for 20 minutes, three times a week, MindFit's proponents believe you can help keep your brain healthy.

Is this the latest in a long line of mental workout tools that play on our fears of the future? Or is there a basis for believing that computer games are good for our brains? And what about the wider hopes that games can improve our minds? Do games teach us to think in ways that better match today's multitasking culture? Or, on the flipside, are they making us less truly intelligent, unable to reflect on anything we do?

In this chapter, I look at the latest claims for computer games and the brain. Can they change the way we think – and if they can, what do we think about that?

MindFit helps keep your brain healthy, it's claimed, by exercising 14 mental faculties.

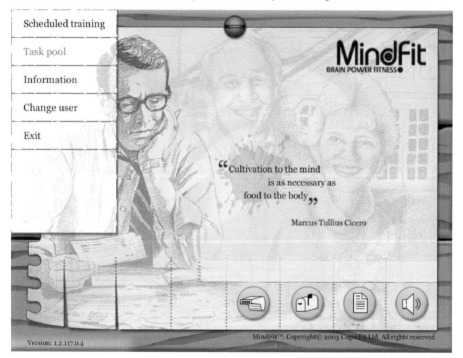

Scheduled training

Task pool

Information

Change user

Exit

MindFit
BRAIN POWER FITNESS●

" Cultivation to the mind
is as necessary as
food to the body "

Marcus Tullius Cicero

Version: 1.2.117.0.4

The Age of the Gaming Granny

Your granny might never have waggled a joystick in anger, but today, 'grey' gaming is huge. If MindFit is seeking players among growing numbers of middle-aged people and elderly folk who are concerned about their faculties and willing to give computer games a try, then it's probably onto a winner.

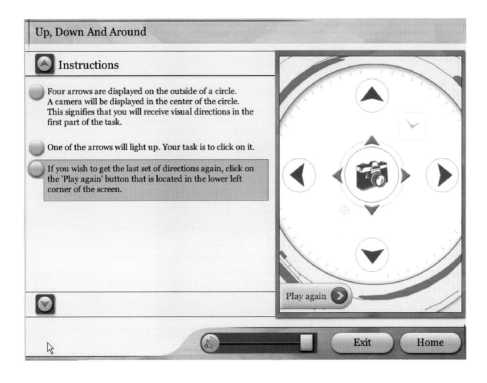

Your granny might never have waggled a joystick in anger, but today, "grey" gaming is huge

The current craze for brain-training games grew up in Japan, where the ageing population has grown to record proportions. There are now classes you can take in Japan to initiate yourself, as BBC Japan correspondent Chris Hogg told me: 'I went to a computer games class in a community centre. The youngest people were in their 50s, and most were newly retired. Everyone sat at desks in groups of 5 and they all had PlayStation Portables. The guy teaching went through it really simply: "This is how you switch it on", and everyone pressed the button. First he taught them how to use brain training software and then a golf game. They seemed to enjoy it.'

Japan's love of modern technology extends to its elderly people too.

PHOTOGRAPH BY DANIEL T. YARA

These new-found game enthusiasts don't sound doddery in the least. And for those in good health, there's no sense of acting your age in Japan. 'There are amazing old people in Japan and they run around in an extremely sprightly way', says Chris. 'It's very different in Britain. I'm not sure my grandmother would have been seen dead at a class like that. Here it is somehow simpler – people aren't worried about how it looks.'

But the craze for brain-training games seems to show that Japanese society is worried about the cognitive decline that can accompany ageing. 'There's been a lot in the papers about exercising your grey matter', Chris tells me. 'No one really knows how to stave off dementia, so in the absence of anything firm, people will believe anyone who tells them something will help. In Japan, if everyone else is doing it, you want to do it too.'

But how much can computer games really help with retaining your ability to think, judge or remember? Is software that focuses on your cognitive abilities any more than a craze that will soon be discredited? And is all the software fundamentally the same?

Mental Gymnastics

The most well-known games for those concerned about their ageing facul-ties are those such as Brain Age: Train your Brain in Minutes a Day for the hand-held Nintendo DS. Brain Age offers to 'give your brain the workout it needs' through a range of activities like maths problems, memory games, Sudoku and logic puzzles. It's been a colossal success in Japan and the craze has spread to more than 10 million daily users around the world.

Nintendo doesn't claim any detailed scientific basis for its brain games, beyond saying the activities stimulate the grey matter by increasing blood flow to the prefrontal cortex. 'We're not claiming it does any more than keep the mind active while letting people have fun', spokeswoman Amber McCollum told a medical news reporter. This hasn't stopped several Japanese hospitals from installing Nintendo DS machines for patients to use while on the wards or in the waiting room.

Brain Age is rather like mental jogging for the hip-replacement generation – although thousands of much younger people use it too. And one reason it's grown so popular in Japan is because of a fundamental sense that games are good for keeping your brain active. Chris Hogg again: 'I visited an old people's home, where they have game machines, exactly the same that you see in an arcade. One of the games was the fairground game where you bash things with a hammer when they pop up. Another one, which was really popular, is where you have two Taiko drums and sticks. It plays a melody and you have to hit the drums: there is no cynicism, it's just great fun.' I hope I'm playing the bongos when I'm in my dotage.

❚❚ I visited an old people's home, where **they have game machines**, exactly the same that you **see** in an arcade **❚❚**

And as the world's population turns ever more silvery-haired, the games industry is looking for ways to benefit. 'When I spoke to Namco, who supplied the games, they said it's part of a strategy to target elderly people, the only section of the market that's growing', explained Chris. 'All games companies are looking to try to expand gaming from just enthusiasts.'

It would perhaps be just as well if we didn't all go into a steep decline once we hit retirement. Can brain training help keep us sharp? Recent research gives a pretty convincing thumbs-up. The *Journal of the American Medical Association* published results in December 2006 from a study among over 2800 over-65s. It showed that those who had taken a short training course to improve memory, reasoning or speed-of-processing showed improved cognitive abilities up to 5 years later.

And even if people's mental faculties have already started to decline, brain games may help re-hone skills. In a 6-month pilot study conducted in Iowa, USA, participants played regular sessions of Happy Neuron games, a set of web-based games designed to give consistent brain-training in memory, language, concentration and reasoning. As part of an overall 'brain wellness program', participants also undertook regular social interaction, physical exercise and ate a low-fat diet with anti-oxidant supplements. Even among 10 participants who'd been diagnosed with memory problems as a probable early sign of Alzheimer's disease, the results were impressive. Those who complied with the protocols of the study (did the others forget?) showed vast improvement in cognitive skills. The positron emission tomography (PET) scans from before and after proved it, revealing increased brain activity. One man even seemed to show 'recovery' of brain activity in his scans, clinical examination and the reports from friends and family.

Evidence from earlier years includes a ground-breaking 1986 study which used the classic arcade game Crystal Castles to try to improve hand–eye coordination in elderly people. Two men and nine women played the game twice a week for 2 months, guiding protagonist Bentley Bear around increasingly tricky-to-navigate castles in search of gems. After such faithful game-training, it's not surprising to learn that the participants' game performance increased significantly. But the players also scored much more highly on a set of tasks that tested perception and motor skills than they had done before gameplay. The men and women who'd taken part reported improved coordination, better driving and fewer minor accidents at home.

So there are studies in the scientific literature that show games may be able to tackle some aspects of mental decline. There are also plenty of examples of games that improve various physical skills, and attributes like sight (see Chapter 1, 'Can Computer Games Affect Your Health?'). But MindFit offers a different approach from other brain-training software, as well as games that are really just for fun. It claims to exercise 14 brain-skills including divided attention, working memory, planning and spatial perception – more than any other similar product. And by giving you a personalised series of tasks to complete at each training session, it selectively targets the areas where you may be starting to slip, or could improve with additional training. 'The biggest difference with MindFit is that it is targeted and personalised', Baroness Greenfield told me after her presentation.

> The biggest **difference** with *MindFit* is that **it is targeted** and **personalised**

Evidence to Keep You Fit

What's the evidence for claims that MindFit is a better bet than other brain-trainers? The study that the company cites was carried out in Israel where the software was originally developed. One hundred twenty-one volunteers aged 50 or over participated in a double-blind clinical trial at Ichilov Hospital, Tel Aviv. Over a 2-year period, they each played either MindFit or various computer games thought to exercise cognitive skills – for example, Tetris.

The results were interesting in two ways. For starters, *all* the participants' brain skills improved. Structured gameplay seemed to have a positive impact on everyone's cognitive abilities. But the participants who played the MindFit games saw a significantly greater improvement: 15% better short-term memory, 19% faster reaction times compared with pre-trial tests, and so on.

'It's like going to a mental gym', says Nittai Hofshi, who's the Vice President for Product Development and R&D for MindFit. 'There's an evaluation phase to create your "cognitive profile". Then a bank of tasks is used to create a training schedule specifically for you. The software recognises how you cope with the task, and gives you personalised feedback.' There's also no getting away with practising only your favourite tasks. MindFit makes sure you're getting a rounded mental education.

In a test carried out by the *Wall Street Journal*, nine people with professional or academic interest in ageing tested out six products aimed at improving brain performance, including MindFit, Happy Neuron, Brain Age and My Brain Trainer. Each product had its own idiosyncrasies that the panel either enjoyed or found frustrating (the evaluation period for MindFit was felt to be too long, for example). But MindFit emerged as the preferred product: it was the most fun, and it seemed to be based on the best research. One tester said that MindFit 'was based the most solidly in cognitive science and what we think stimulates the brain'.

The personal feedback and carefully phrased instructions are particularly tailored to an audience aged 50-plus, according to Nittai Hofshi. And another factor in making the game user-friendly is the lack of a sense of being compared to anyone else. 'There's no normative grade – we are not measuring IQ', explained Hofshi. You improve relative to yourself alone, so there's no risk, as one of the testers of another product for the *Wall Street Journal* found, of being told she was 'slow and below average'.

Our mental **faculties** start to decline from around the **age of 20**

Might not the prospect of competition with others inspire some players? It's apparently a topic of hot debate among the MindFit team. And what about trying out the games on younger people? It could be done. 'Our mental faculties do start to decline from around the age of 20', says Hofshi. It might take some redesigning to make the games child-appropriate, but perhaps MindFit's approach would provide some children with a welcome break from the grade-oriented environment of school.

How Does Brain Training Work, If It Works?

The way in which brain-training games may work is based in relatively new science. For years, scientists believed you were born with all the neurons you'd ever have – and your brain went downhill from there as they naturally died off or were killed by life's onslaught of hormones, alcohol, caffeine and stress (fun!). Now we know otherwise: *neurogenesis*, the creation of new neurons, takes place all your life.

Neuroscientist Tracey Shors at Rutgers University shed more light on the process of neurogenesis in an email to me: 'We have seen in studies of mammals that thousands of cells are produced each day in the hippocampus, a structure of the brain that is used for many types of learning and memory. The number produced does depend to some extent on the environment. For example, a more stimulating environment induces the birth of more new cells in the hippocampus.' So the brain is producing new cells – good news. But it appears that they won't necessarily 'stick'.

'We find that most of the new cells die within weeks, unless the animals learn something new. However, not all types of learning are effective – rather it seems that the more demanding the task, the more likely that the cells will survive. Once rescued from death, the vast majority turn into neurons and seem to remain in the brain indefinitely.'

Can we apply these findings to human brains? 'The effect of learning on neurogenesis has not been shown in humans', warns Shors. 'That said, there is no

We now know the mammalian brain (shown here) produces thousands of new cells each day in the hippocampus. But you have to work them hard to make them survive.

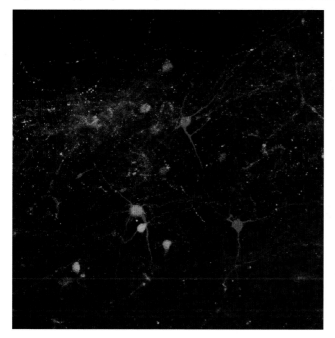

❝❝ A more **stimulating** environment **induces the birth** of more **new cells** in the hippocampus ❞❞

reason to believe that the process would be different. We mammals are, after all, much more similar than we are different.' So our best information is that human brains produce new cells, and that we can put them to good use by using them for demanding tasks. It's the old 'use it or lose it' adage.

Lata Aiman, who studies the cognitive effects of computer games at Deakin University, Melbourne, Australia, is a little sceptical about hyped press claims made for brain-training software. 'With regard to improving certain skills, perhaps games could assist; however, there is not much research to support this', she counsels. 'The important thing with the development of such games is that they be developed in line with the principles of the particular skill they are trying to enhance and also that they be tried and tested in a rigorous manner before being sold in the market and making the claims they do.'

Exercises for Mind and Body

As populations age, dementia will rocket in the next three decades, experts estimated recently in *The Lancet*. Today, more than 24 million people have dementia, but by 2040 that number could reach 81 million – with the most common form Alzheimer's disease. To keep brains toned and honed, it appears that activities requiring complex thinking are needed. Anything too easy might not make much difference – it's tackling new problems that seems to do the trick.

Today, **more than 24 million** people have **dementia,** but by **2040** that number could reach **81 million**

How do games measure up alongside more traditional forms of grey entertainment? Medical advice has long recommended regular exercise as beneficial to elderly people (thank you, Sherlock) because of the overall improvement in blood flow and brain health. But when it comes to warding off Alzheimer's disease, there are now more specific findings. A 21-year-long study published in the *New England Journal of Medicine* in 2003 compared physical and mental activities in the over-75s, looking for evidence of their efficacy in preventing Alzheimer's. Among the physical diversions, dancing was the only one that led to reduced risk of the disease in over 450 elderly people who were part of the study. 'Dancing isn't purely physical, it involves some mental effort', explained lead researcher Joe Verghese. 'Climbing stairs and walking are more automatic as far as the brain is concerned.'

With the mentally stimulating activities, the picture was very different. Reading, cards and board games, crossword puzzles, and playing a musical instrument all appeared to ward off the damage of disease. Those who enjoyed such brain-boosting activities about 4 days a week were two thirds less likely to get Alzheimer's, the study showed.

It's crucial to get a balance of both mental and physical activity – that seems to be the take-home message. Professor Michael Kirby is an expert in health and human sciences at the University of Hertfordshire. On the day I spoke to him he'd been swimming at 7 a.m., and normally plans for an evening cycle-ride or walk on his return home. 'Society has been preoccupied with staying fit, but many people think it's just about taking a vitamin pill', he said. 'You need to exercise your mind as well as your body – that's the way to add life to years, rather than just years to life.'

Whatever the long-term findings show, current research gives weight to the idea that brain training might reap real rewards for those of us wanting to nourish our ageing neurons and give them a workout that will result in being able to find our keys (and marbles) long into our twilight years.

Don't Computer Games Rot Your Brain?

The accusation that most ordinary computer games cause brain rot is still extremely common. When I asked people what their friends and family thought

Cards and board games help ward off Alzheimer's disease.

PHOTOGRAPH BY DAISUKE

about the games they played, many said their gaming was sadly misunderstood. Chris, 29, said his family 'wondered why he played games at his age', while a 39-year-old gamer felt his family and friends thought game-playing was 'a bit sad'. Wai Yin, 19, said that 'family members, especially my mom, think it's a waste of time'. Judy, aged 60, said 'Son Jonathan thinks it's great; husband considers all games a waste of time; daughter occasionally partakes.' Michael, 29, of Durham was one of very few who said his family and friends were: 'not fussed . . . It seems we are in a gaming culture now, where playing games doesn't class you as a "nerd".' People in the north of England are obviously an enlightened lot.

A sense that digital technology is encroaching on every corner of life is not one that everyone thinks is good. Even Baroness Susan Greenfield has expressed concern that technology may be dumbing us down, even as it speeds things up. In a speech to the House of Lords in 2006, she pointed out the different 'information landscape' in which children are now growing up, in which, for example, the Internet has made memorising facts less relevant. What effect could this be having on our short-term or long-term memory skills?

And the fact that children now learn less from reading by themselves, or from traditional teaching mediated by a mentor is also a worry. 'When we of the twentieth century read a book', said Baroness Greenfield in her speech, 'usually the author takes you by the hand and you travel from the beginning to the middle to the end in a continuous narrative series of interconnected steps . . . we can then of course compare one narrative with another. In so doing we start to build up a conceptual framework that enables us to evaluate further journeys, which in turn will influence our individualised framework.'

For Baroness Greenfield, this is the basis of education: the building of personalised mental maps to help us understand the context and significance of each new piece of information. At the launch of MindFit, she acknowledged the power of computers for learning how to see patterns and make connections.

'For kids, [computers] are a wonderful facility but they must be harnessed', she said.

It certainly seems valid that the availability of a hugely powerful medium like the Internet will change the way we conduct learning – although traditional schooling may take time to incorporate this resource most effectively. But is it changing the way we think?

Marc Prensky thinks it already has. An international consultant on learning and technology, he's recognised a new generation of Digital Natives, the people who have grown up with computers, games, mobile phones and broadband connectivity as part of everyday life. It's his view that, having spent more hours in their lives playing computer games than reading, these people literally think differently from those who went before.

And Prensky points out that the repeated, focused activity required by many brain-training games is exactly what countless people have been doing for years through ordinary game-playing (see box, 'Are Computer Games Making Us Smarter'?).

David Jay Bolter, a professor of language, communication and culture at Georgia Institute of Technology, has a unique perspective on the effect that technology has been having on our thinking. He was one of the early proponents of hypertext – the linking of web pages through highlighted words. In a 2001 interview he marvelled at the acceptance that the Internet had found in America's schools, compared with the reception of other new media – photography, film, radio and television. 'There is a near consensus that computers belong in schools, that schools should be hooked to the Internet, and that students should be given access to the Web and in many cases should learn to create their own Web pages', he said.

But the resulting effects Bolter predicted have been very different to those he's observed since, as he told me when we spoke. He used to speculate that the ubiquity of networked computers in education could result in a 'hypertextual' style of writing – death of the narrative essay and the narrative way of teaching. He also saw a threat to verbal literacy from the emphasis placed on images on the Internet. 'American education has been principally verbal for centuries . . . I'm not predicting that verbal literacy will cease to be important, but I do think that visual literacy may begin to claim a place in our educational programs.' So what's come true – and has anything changed?

Reports of the death of narrative had been greatly exaggerated, according to Bolter in 2007. 'No one is encouraging students to write hypertext essays', he told me. 'If you look at traditional education, teaching writing, say, it hasn't changed much in the past twenty years in its basic assumptions about the way communication should work. We envisioned a new form of literary communication, argument and discourse that would grow up. It hasn't happened – people are still using computers to write traditional articles and essays – and some people are disappointed.'

If hypertext thinking is more natural – a better match to our own cognitive style – then haven't we lost something important? Bolter isn't dogmatic about his former views. 'Some people claim it's more natural but I'm sceptical of that now. I think each form of communication does something better than other forms. People still read linear novels – look at the frenzy over knowing what happened at the end of the *Harry Potter* series. It's very seldom that one form of media gets totally replaced.'

And since his 2001 interview there have been fascinating new developments: 'Students are now using technology outside the classroom in new ways. The year 2001 pre-dated a whole host of phenomena that come under the heading of social computing. MySpace, FaceBook, YouTube – their characteristics are very different to what we predicted. They don't have academic sanction: they exist outside the teaching rubric, which is part of their appeal.'

What difference are these new applications making? 'It's a very fragmented form of communication', says Bolter. 'You write these little notes and messages, you create networks of friends, you communicate not only verbally, but visually, and with audio. It's eclectic and postmodern – not much to do with any of the traditional rules and practices we try to teach at school.'

So on this point, Bolter's 2001 crystal ball-gazing was right – imagery has become increasingly important. Without visuals, and the computer power to animate them, YouTube and FaceBook don't mean much. And in computer games, powerful technology for virtual worlds and interactions are opening up new possibilities, too.

In terms of thinking skills, Bolter sees changes ahead. 'We'll be richer for the new opportunities offered by technology. But we usually end up sacrificing something. People aren't going to be writing such powerful essays, perhaps, but we'll be better at gathering information and looking at its relevance. There's a trade-off.'

We usually **end up sacrificing something. People** aren't going to be **writing such powerful essays,** but we'll be **better** at **gathering information** and looking at its relevance

Are Computer Games Making Us Smarter?

Can games really benefit your brain? Before you reach anywhere near your decline, games could help sharpen your thinking at critical times, as the following scientific findings show:

- In 1987, researchers investigated children's skill at mentally rotating 3-D objects, correlating the data with their gaming experience. Those who played computer games consistently out-thought their non-gaming contemporaries at age 10, 12 and 15.
- In 1994, Tetris was proven to improve players' ability to visualise and manipulate shapes after 6 hours' play. The same year, psychologists showed that playing The Empire Strikes Back, which involves navigating through 3-D spaces, led to improvements in mental paper-folding tasks.
- Marble Madness was the game of choice for research in 1996. One group of 12-year-olds manoeuvred marbles through an isometric cityscape against the clock. Another group played word-puzzle game Conjecture. After two and a half hours' play, the marble manipulators had significantly improved their mental skills, while Conjecture had no such benefit.

How might those skills be of use? Don't imagine Tetris leads to shelf-stacking – think architecture, engineering, air traffic control – all professions that require highly developed skills in mental modelling and three-dimensional thinking.

Could Tetris help develop skills in the kind of mental modelling needed for air traffic control?

Smartening Up in Today's World

In his book *Everything Bad Is Good for You,* journalist Steven Johnson tackles the prevailing idea that popular culture is brain rot. His thesis is that mass culture is much more sophisticated and challenging than ever before, providing what he calls 'positive brainwashing' that makes our minds sharper as we take it in.

Johnson presents evidence that cognitive benefits come from playing computer games – whether you're 7 or 70 years old. 'Far more than books or movies or music, games force you to make decisions', says Johnson in a chapter on games.

'Novels may activate our imagination, and music may conjure up powerful emotions, but games force you to decide, to choose, to prioritize.' Far from simply learning to push buttons faster or shoot straighter, games ask you to weigh evidence, analyse situations, consult long-term goals and then plump for one action or another: pure brainwork.

In my survey, many people referred to cognitive challenge in describing the benefit or enjoyment the experienced in a particular game.

Has this game improved your life in any way? 'I doubt it, other than keeping the brain alive (see age!)' (Paul, 60, who plays the solitaire card game Freecell)

'I like how quest and puzzle are integrated, the pattern recognition aspect, the emergent challenges.' (Kristine, 29, Puzzle Quest – a game that combines puzzles with a role-playing environment)

'The thing I like most is the logical thinking of MineSweeper. If I was having difficulty getting started with the writing [of my dissertation], I would use the game to kickstart my brain.' (Cathie, 44)

'Building systems and watching how they work is soothing to me. I like to experiment with different configurations without having to worry whether or not I'm winning.' (Alice, 34, SimCity, a city-building simulation game)

'I'm absolutely convinced that the last decade of Tomb Raider games has improved my spatial awareness and mapping abilities in the "real world".' (Barry, 37, author of The Rough Guide to the Brain)

And all this brainwork is definitely having an effect. Back in 1992 Richard Haier and colleagues at the University of California at Irvine investigated the effects of Tetris on the brain. They asked 24 men to play the game every day for up to 8 weeks, during which time their performance improved seven-fold. Haier used brain scans to monitor the men's brain glucose metabolism over the period – a way of measuring how much energy the brain was using to perform the task at hand. He found that after performance in the game improved, the test subjects' brains required much less glucose to continue playing. Their brains had worked out more efficient ways of achieving the results.

While learning to play the game, the authors believed that the men were trying out many different cognitive approaches. But once the game was familiar, the lowering of glucose levels 'reflects a more selective use of brain circuitry, reflecting a better-honed cognitive strategy' for playing the game. They no longer had to break into a mental sweat.

Can Players Really Transfer Game Skills to Real Life?

Cognitive benefits to playing computer games are all well and good. But how can we be sure that any of the painstakingly acquired screen skills are transferred to daily life? I put the question to Lata Aiman at Deakin University. 'I think gamers do gain cognitive skills that make them more successful in real life tasks, based on my research so far', she confirmed. 'When I tested performance on a divided attention task, I used tasks that were external, not performance on the game itself. Participants' improvement in performing the test task showed that the skills they had acquired playing the game could transfer to external tasks.' Aiman is convinced the same applied to her reaction-time results. However, she warned me of the need to keep up the gameplay to continue seeing the cognitive benefits. 'I think an adequate amount of practice or training on a consistent basis is required for the skills to remain "improved" and assist with tasks in real life.'

Our own brains are, of course, often way ahead of us in realising when there's a chance to pick up some useful skills. Research published in 2001 found real-life cognitive benefits of a golf simulation game – even when there was no direct reason for them to be there. Scientists at the René Descartes University, Paris, tested two groups of players with a computer golf game. The researchers had chosen the game to be an accurate visual simulation of golf, but with no bodily feedback whatsoever. The funny thing was that, despite no physical training having taken place, golfers who tried the computer game nonetheless improved their control of force when putting on real-life greens. Especially interesting – nay, amazing – was the finding that some who said they could sense the 'force of the virtual player's putting swing' while playing the game showed some of the largest improvement in actual putting performance.

The results were **so impressive** that the **Israeli flight school** incorporated the software into the **training** programme for **all recruits**

The key to reproducing game-learnt skills in real-life situations seems to be making the game tasks *cognitively* similar to life, rather than necessarily *visually* similar. That's the message from Israel Institute of Technology's Daniel Gopher, who's rather a guru in this area. Back in 1994 he wrote a ground-breaking article published in the *Human Factors* journal about how he'd found computer-game training transferred to real life for pilots. After training flight cadets for 10 hours in the game Space Fortress, Gopher demonstrated a 30% improvement in their flight performance. The results were so impressive that the Israeli flight school incorporated the software into the training programme for all recruits. US flight training now also includes game training.

'Traditional approaches [to training simulators] focus on physical fidelity, which may seem more intuitive, but is less effective and harder to achieve', Professor Gopher told Sharpbrains – a brain-science consultancy and proponent of brain fitness – in February 2007. 'What we have discovered is that a key factor for an effective transfer from training environment to reality is that the training program ensures *cognitive fidelity*, that is, it should faithfully represent the mental demands that happen in the real world.'

Professor Gopher is a cognitive psychologist with particular interests in how to expand the limits of human attention, information processing and response capabilities in extremely complex and demanding tasks – say, for example, flying a military jet. He says that the pursuit of realism in software developed for training purposes is a red herring. 'The need for physical fidelity is not based on research, at least for the type of high-performance training we are talking about', he told Sharpbrains. 'In fact, a simple environment may be better in that it does not create the illusion of reality.' In support of this view, Gopher published research sponsored by NASA in 1992, comparing his Space Fortress cognitive trainer with a sophisticated graphical and physical simulator of a Black Hawk helicopter. While the former – with its basic line-drawn graphics – improved performance, the costly latter option did not.

The Multi-tasking Masters

In 2003, psychologist Lata Aiman used the whimsical action-adventure game Banjo Kazooie in a study. She wanted to investigate a different kind of cognitive benefit: the ability to multitask. 'The players in my study were not habitual game players', Aiman told me. 'Their average age was just under 20 years, and almost half of them considered their ability to play video games "average" or "worse than average".' After they had played the game, participants were asked to perform two complex processes simultaneously, such as encoding and retrieving words while performing a concurrent reaction time task. Sounds tricky? Despite the test subjects' lack of confidence, gameplay still improved their ability to juggle tasks. Those who had played Banjo Kazooie for 6 hours outperformed those who had only played for 1 hour. Aiman saw this as evidence that games can assist with real-life 'divided-attention' tasks such as piloting an aeroplane.

In a second study, Aiman used computer game training in a similar way to see its effect on players' reaction times. Results showed no difference in reaction time for a group who played for 1 hour. But for those that played for 6 hours, reaction times significantly improved.

Daphne Bavelier and Shawn Green at the University of Rochester, New York, came to similar conclusions about multitasking and computer games in 2003. Their experiments showed that an action game like Medal of Honour boosted players' skills at juggling several tasks simultaneously. Tetris had no such benefits as players concentrated on only one task at a time. (Find out more about the duo's findings relating to visual skills in the chapter 'Can Computer Games Affect Your Health?')

How about the kind of games traditionally accused of promoting violence or addictiveness? Well, there's evidence they can also confer improvements in multitasking. Research from Unitec Institute of Technology in Auckland, New Zealand, published in 2005, investigated the effects of the first-person shooter game Counter-Strike on players' abilities to multitask. To gauge this impact, researcher Paul Kearney used a simulated work environment called SynWin, in which you have to keep track of several tasks at once, responding to requests and taking appropriate action.

Two test groups participated in the experiment; one group who rarely played computer games was used as a control group. The control group played SynWin three times, their skill at coordinating their work-like activities improving steadily over the three tests. The test group played SynWin once as a baseline measure, then played Counter-Strike for 2 hours in lab conditions, and then played SynWin again. This group found that the game did indeed increase their ability to multitask. Rather than the experiment just using a computer game (SynWin) to measure the effect of a computer game (Counter-Strike), Kearney saw that 'the immersive environment created by Counter-Strike captivated the attention of the players ... the participants were completely focused on the game.' He concluded that the ability to multitask and focus on several things at once is imperative in the real-life workplace, and that the game actively helped in achieving this.

No Time to Think?

Games may be training our brains to process streams of conflicting information, but what if, as David Jay Bolter suggests, we are losing other skills in the
process? Another of Baroness Susan Greenfield's concerns is that the multi-
channel, multimedia world in which we live is leaving no time to think. As she said
in her House of Lords speech: 'The sounds and sights of a fast-paced, fast-moving
multimedia presentation would displace any time for reflection or any idiosyn-
cratic or imaginative connections that we might make as we turn the pages, then
stare at the wall to reflect.'

Reflection might not appear to be one of the main aspects of computer gameplay.
And yet the idea that people who've grown up with games can only do one thing
at once is being challenged. We've seen that some games actively train players
to deal efficiently with competing tasks clamouring for their attention. And perhaps
we can conclude that the current and future generations of Digital Natives will
have a different way of coping, cognitively, with the world they find.

The **current and future** generations of *Digital
Natives* **will have** a **different** way of coping
cognitively, with the **world** they find

Eric Newton, vice president of the journalism program at the Knight Foundation
in Miami, Florida, has been examining the power of computer games and asking

whether players are developing new kinds of brain patterns or literacies. 'What seems to be changing is the attention span of young people, and the phenomenon of multitasking', he told me. 'If I go into my older son William's room, he is doing homework on a laptop, he's keeping up ten instant messenger (IM) conversations on the main computer, he's paying an electric guitar, and listening to the radio. And then he says 'How come there's no TV in here?' He's IM-ing about what he's playing on the guitar or what's on the radio, commenting on the homework. Someone else IMs about a television programme but he can't see it because there's no TV in the room.'

This ability to juggle so many inputs is what's labelled 'continuous partial attention' by computing pioneer Linda Stone, who coined the phrase in 1997. By paying continuous partial attention, we keep the top-level item in focus and scan the periphery in case something more important emerges. Stone sees this as a 'post-multitasking' behaviour – a way to cope in a sea of overwhelming responsibilities and relationships that is complicated further by the addition of virtual communities, social networks and 24-hour online friendships.

A clever way to keep all the balls in the air? Or a shaky foundation for a fulfilled life? Stone seems to believe the latter. 'Continuous partial attention isn't motivated by productivity, it's motivated by being connected', she said in a 2005 presentation. Being connected makes us feel alive, but simultaneously, 'lack of meaning underscores how promiscuous and how empty this way of life made us feel.' The way out, Stone believes, is to use technology as a gatekeeper to pick the good stuff to which we can pay full attention.

But what if our minds are adapting to cope with the way we live now? The next generation – the gaming generation of which Eric Newton's son is a member – may have developed skills that make this frenetic-looking activity perfectly meaningful.

Jon Sykes, a psychologist and computer-games lecturer at Glasgow Caledonian University, thinks this could be true. 'When you surf the net, you might have eight different tabs open, eight different conversations going with the internet. And you can keep all these going in your head. Someone forty years ago would have found that impossible, and now a kid of six can do it, no problem.'

Sykes suggests we may be developing rules and skills without even realising we're doing it. 'There's a massive stream of information around us, but we may be instinctively working out how to cope with it and decide efficiently what it is important at that moment. I have a system in my office, for example, where I put work down on my desk. It all piles up and if someone comes in and draws my attention to something in the pile, it comes to the top. If no one's bothered me about it, I guess it isn't that important. I clear my desk once a year and I've never had a problem with forgetting anything crucial.'

Are we developing new rules for organising our busy lives?

Conclusion

Do you train your brain? I put this question to Michael Kirby, the health and human sciences professor, when I was interviewing him. He didn't say yes, or no, but pointed to his daily schedule of diagnosis, research, working out drug dosages and talking to people. 'I get forced to use my brain because I am faced with problems every day', he says, in the voice of someone who genuinely loves his job.

He's probably one of the rare people who do use the full range of their brainpower in their daily lives. But most of us specialise pretty early on into things we are good at, or things we find easy – why wouldn't we? We neglect certain activities because we're told we're not talented at it; because we think we can't do it, or because we simply forget what else is out there in the rush of everyday life. The evidence seems to say that a product like MindFit that promises to exercise all our mental faculties might do us some serious good. And who knows: 14 ways to train your brain may be excessive; the other products that claim to exercise five or seven skills may also be valuable, as long as you choose a good variety of games.

Among the over-50s, a **fifth** already play a **computer game** at least **once a week** to keep their **brain ticking over**

'Fun' computer games may be working on our brains, even if we don't realise. The cognitive advantages of computer games should give them the same cultural significance as crosswords or Sudoku – and I'd rather play Tetris any day instead of filling in numbers in a square. But evidently lots of people already know that.

Even among the over-50s, a fifth already play a computer game at least once a week to keep their brain ticking over – according to a UK survey in 2007.

Then there's the idea that we are getting smarter just by using modern media, and by coping with the juggle of tasks that would have driven earlier generations to distraction. I enjoy the 'fuzzy' idea by which Jon Sykes organises his desk – or is it just because mine is always piled with stuff, too?

So, would you try MindFit? Now that I know more about its basis in science I just might. It would mean dropping something else from the schedule, though – and that would be hard to justify. There may be more pressing calls on the few spare minutes in the day: I'm just trying to remember the last time I did any 'swimming', 'running' or any of the other necessary physical activities Professor Kirby mentioned. And our piano is looking forlornly at me. Was I going to finish that game of Riven sometime? Visit Venice before it sinks? When did I last go to the cinema? Did I once say that I was going to learn Chinese? MindFit – I might have to get back to you.

3 Can Computer Games Change Who You Are?

Introduction

Plumber, physicist, gun-toting archaeologist, gangster, soldier, refugee, princess, rock star, micro-sized car . . . or even God. Who are you when you're playing a game?

Are you a sprite on a screen – a way of interacting in the game, and no more? Maybe you take on roles – hitman, Halfling, hedgehog – that you'd never get to fulfil in real life. Or, if you play in online worlds, do you spend hours designing and perfecting the ideal 'you' to present to the cybercommunity?

Whether we like it or not, research shows that the games you play affect the person you are. Games can help you win friends, and learn to influence people. They can reveal your personality through your decision to create an online character that's attractive, tall or wearing certain colours. And they may even be able to expose your deep-held attitudes in matters of bad behaviour: racism, torture, bullying, dangerous driving and cheating.

Your avatar – your virtual character – can say a lot about who you are online. These images show variations on the same character in the world There

Games may even be **able to expose** your **deep-held** attitudes in **matters of bad behaviour:** racism, **torture, bullying,** dangerous driving and **cheating**

When it comes to character, we're complex creatures. Science is a long way from understanding all that we do. But the underlying question with which researchers are wrestling is this: can we decode what we do in real life by looking at how we play games? Can we understand our game-behaviour by looking at what we do in reality? And if we don't pay more attention to the powerful ways in which games can affect our personalities, what are the risks we run?

Do Games Make Us Sociable?

It's that terrible old stereotype again: the gamer sitting alone in his room (it's always a him), glued to the computer or console, neither moving nor interacting for hours or days at a time. OK – some people have an addiction to gaming, but it's extremely rare (see Chapter 4, 'Can Computer Games Turn You into an Addict?'). What if we were to find that for the majority, games were extremely sociable activities?

There was plenty of evidence in my survey that people loved games for their ability to provide social cohesion and fun. For many, games were a cultural crossing point that provided common references – like any cultural activity from East-enders to Chinese New Year. 'It's good fun playing against housemates – the competition, the wine-drinking', reported Annie, 40, describing cartoon-style platform game Crash Bandicoot.

> **▌▌ I** know that **I** would have a **relationship with my brothers without** games, **too**, but **I** wonder if it would **be as good** ▐▐

Another respondent explained what a difference a game had made to his sibling relationships: 'I have three brothers, and all of us live in different towns in Finland', said Marko, 29. 'We have frequent contact with one another anyway, but I feel that playing [turn-based strategy] games such as Space Empires together adds a nice layer to our "normal" communication.' There is a 12-year age span between the four brothers, and games have provided a significant bonding experience in periods when they had little else in common. 'Speaking about the game at hand, or the game to be, planning and plotting with allies, divulging false information at oppor-tune times when sitting at the same coffee table at the parents' house – all of this is a way of keeping up the connection. I know that I would have a relationship with my brothers without games, too, but I wonder if it would be as good.'

One respondent to my survey noted that he spent an entire evening once playing the cerebral turn-based strategy game Civilization instead of going to a party that was taking place downstairs from his room. To those at the party it must have looked like the decision of a true dweeb. But he was at a different party – the one happening in his online game. And others have remarked on the power of their network of game-friends.

Dan, 42, said 'The most outstanding experiences [in World of Warcraft] have been on the social side rather than the gameplay side, for example one of our guild members having a child, another going through bereavement, another struggling with depression, and seeing the support the social network has provided.' A 40-year-old online gamer told me 'I had an online "best friend" who passed away last spring. It was heart-wrenching. Amazing to never have met in person but still feel horribly sad that your friend is gone.'

There are many stories – nay, legends – of how online games have changed people's lives. Friends and online acquaintances of Mona Cyclona, a well-known leader in the virtual world There, were surprised and saddened to learn of her real-life death in 2003. Slowly her story emerged – from birth she'd suffered from brittle bone disease that severely limited her height, and restricted every activity – apart from that of participating in computer games, where she'd risen to the top in a way she never could in 'real life'.

In June 2004, a US woman barricaded herself in an upper bedroom to escape an attack by her violent husband. With only her computer on hand, she logged in and sent an SOS to all her gaming buddies, asking one of them to call the police. Four timezones away, an in-world friend saw the message and called both the police and the woman's mother who lived locally. Help was soon dispatched.

According to Professor Mark Griffiths, a psychologist at Nottingham Trent University, online gaming is indeed an 'extremely social' activity. His research published in 2007 combined the experiences of over 900 gamers from 45 countries, of average age 23.6 years. And they were a very sociable lot. 81% said they played their online game with real-life friends and family. Three quarters of gamers reported making good friends with people they met online. Forty percent chose to discuss sensitive issues with online friends.

Online gaming is **indeed** an **"extremely social"** activity

And for many people, online friendship led to real-life meetings, and more. Thirty percent of the survey respondents said they'd been attracted to someone else online. Almost half had actually met up with people they'd met online – with 1 in 10 going on to develop physical relationships. In my survey, Jo, 51, said that he'd met his real-life girlfriend via the game There, and that they now live in nearby cities.

Almost half had **actually met up** with people they'd **met** online – with **one in ten** going on to develop **physical** relationships

Games that offer a 3-D world to explore and a personal avatar to customise are perhaps especially involving. 'Because you have a body, it's much more intimate and real and it's only a matter of time before you find someone you really click with', says Theresa, a veteran of the online world Second Life. 'Lots of relationships form and they are very deep. Real life marriages come out, and they seem pretty strong'.

For some people, inevitably, this means conflict between the game-world and the rest of life. Does it mean that people leave their real-life partners behind? 'It is a danger zone in many respects, and it disrupts real life. But I think Second Life saves as many marriages as it collapses. I think those that don't survive are doomed anyway', Theresa says.

Her own relationship was on the rocks when she started playing Second Life. 'We had been apart for almost two years. And during that time I learned some things through Second Life that made me look at my marriage and think "do I want to be here in five years?" I wanted more.' Theresa is now divorced and lives with her 13-year-old son, of whom she says: 'Overall, he's seen a mom who's had the courage to really live.' She's gone from being a woman whose husband wanted her 'frozen in time', to an entrepreneur with 17 members of staff and three design businesses.

The online gamers who replied to my survey were all very positive about the social side of their virtual world. But for some, it didn't cross over into real life, perhaps because their online friends lived too far away. For another, the game made her feel connected to the world because real life is 'segmented, not even knowing your neighbour a lot of times'.

We won't have **"friends from my online world"** and "friends I know from work/**school**/the pub". **We'll just have friends**

Is it common to experience a rift between the online world and the real world – two separate existences with no cross-over at all? Mark Griffiths says no. 'For people who inhabit both worlds, I don't think there ever was a rift. Traditionally you've had a technological generation gap, with some people unable to understand why others would want to spend time online', he said. 'With more and more people playing online games, that's now changing. For this generation, forming friend-ships and relationships online won't be strange – this is what human life will be like. It's becoming normalized.'

The big change seems to be that soon, we won't have 'friends from my online world' and 'friends I know from work/school/the pub'. We'll just have friends.

Do Games Help You Influence People?

Games can boost players' confidence, according to my research. One gamer reported 'I would say that winning this game immediately strengthened my self-trust, as anyone who succeeded in completing a hard challenge.' Yin Liang, 21, said that playing futuristic combat game Warhammer 40,000 had shown him that all opponents 'have a weakness and a way to overcome it, I just need the experience and practice . . . which can be applied to real life situations.' Chagall told me 'After I'd been in There a while, I realized I wasn't under anyone's wing. Then I started to realize how I reacted to things on my own and such, forming my own opinions instead of hiding behind someone else's.'

Nic Crowe is an academic from Brunel University who studies how young people use online worlds. He sees lots of positive activity going on in the fantasy online world RuneScape among the 11- to 14-year-olds he researches.

'They learn to run communities as clan leaders', says Nic, describing the virtual teams that work together in RuneScape. 'There are incredible leadership and management skills. One of the leaders is only 16 and she runs one of the fishing guilds.' Fishing is one way you can generate a lot of money in the game. 'One of the rival guilds tried to drop the price of lobsters, so she blockaded the port for 24 hours and brought the lobster-fishing in the area to a standstill to make her point. It was a successful piece of social and political action.'

The game empowers even quite young players, according to Nic. 'Club Penguin is for 5- to 11-year-olds', he says. 'You can buy your penguin a sweater. In real life, those children can't generate their own income, but all of a sudden in that arena they can buy a penguin a pair of sunglasses. The pleasure is the same as for adults.'

Do Games Show Who You Really Are?

When we play games, what does it show about us? Years ago when Multi-User Dungeons (MUD) first emerged – text-based adventure worlds – their creator, Richard Bartle, studied the thousands of people who played them. He classified players into four sub-groups: Achievers, Explorers, Killers and Socialisers. He also observed that each of those types of players perceived the experience in a different way. To achievers it was a game like chess or tennis. To an explorer, it was a pastime like reading or gardening. For killers it was like hunting or fishing. And for a socialiser, the MUD was like a nightclub or other form of entertainment. The question about whether online worlds should be perceived as games continues today.

In 2003, a researcher surveyed contemporary online gameplayers to try to shed light on their psychological make-up, using Bartle's test. Among players of Ever-Quest, the analysis showed that 34% were Explorers, 25% Achievers, 23% Socialisers and 15% Killers. The questions are inevitably reminiscent of 'team-building'

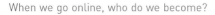
When we go online, who do we become?

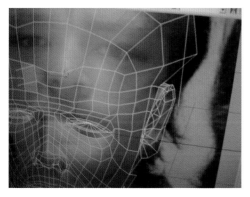

tests taken in the workplace (apart from the sword references) – and indeed the Bartle scores have been mapped to the Myers-Briggs models of personality types often used to shed light on our work personae.

2004 research into how people behave in online worlds showed a majority said they were very similar or fairly similar to real life. More women than men strongly identified with their online persona. Among the over-35s, nearly 70% said they acted as they did normally.

Many gamers agree their on-screen self mirrors their real-life attributes. 'In Warcraft I'm a healer,' says Margaret Robertson. 'I stand at the back, keeping other people alive. I love it. It's an extension of how I approach things in real life. You get to come off like a hero, saving lives without actually taking risks, and I like being able to randomly help people.'

Many gamers agree their on-screen self mirrors their real-life attributes

But couldn't we take on a fantasy personality as we enter a fantasy game-world online? Technology journalist and researcher Aleks Krotoski thinks for most people it's unlikely. 'People use these spaces for self-expression', she says. 'It's too much work to adopt an alternative persona online, you'd go completely insane. You just extend yourself in different ways. Whatever you're doing: learning Photoshop, or building things in 3D, or having a discussion, or going to have cybersex: it is just an extension of yourself. You *are* who you are online.'

▐▐ It's too much work to adopt an alternative persona online, you'd go completely insane ▐▐

Theresa, who runs a business in Second Life, told me more about her in-world persona Tessa. 'I'm integrated with my Second Life personality', she told me. 'Tessa is my goal body – I know I'll never get that thin again but by Second Life standards I'm chunky. Most girls are anorexic with these huge breasts and platform shoes; and you're waiting for them to topple over. You also have your tummy out because that's the way the clothes are made.'

What effect does Tessa's appearance have on the way she interacts? 'In Second Life, our appearances are quite relaxed and revealing. I think there's a psychological impact which is that we communicate on a much more open level. It's ironic because we're in fake bodies with fake hair and skin, and yet we can be more open than we are in real life. That's the irony and the magic of Second Life.'

> We're in **fake bodies** with **fake hair** and **skin**, and **yet we can be more open** than we **are in real life.** That's the **irony** and the **magic** of *Second Life*

Digital Identities

What is research telling us about how our appearance affects our actions? Scientists have known for some time that the way we are perceived can affect our behaviour. Yes – that's right – the way *other people perceive us* can cause us to behave differently. A seminal study in 1977 asked male and female undergraduates to talk to each other on a telephone. The men (the perceivers) were given biographical information about the woman (the target), plus a photo that supposedly pictured her (either an attractive or unattractive photo). The men rated their initial impression of the woman, and then they chatted for 10 minutes.

Pre-chat questionnaires showed clearly that the men who thought they were going to talk to somebody attractive anticipated that the woman would be comparatively sociable, poised, humorous and socially adept. For those given the unattractive photo, the opposite was true. The men tended to reflect these expectations in the way they spoke to the women – either animated and humorous, or awkward and reticent. In turn, the women were observed to respond to the men in a way that fulfilled the men's expectation – either poised or gawky. In other words, the target's behaviour changed solely because of the way the perceiver saw them – an effect called behavioural confirmation.

Nick Yee researches identity and behaviour in online worlds. And in this context – where people's choice of avatar is crucial to their online identity – he has a new way of explaining how we behave. Rather than picking up cues from others' behaviour to know how to behave ourselves, Yee believes that our own perception of our appearance causes us to behave as we think others would expect: a phenomenon he calls the *Proteus Effect*.

Yee, who recently completed a PhD at Stanford University in California, has evidence that this is what's going on. He has run multiple experiments using a virtual reality scenario, in which volunteers are shown a virtual reflection of themselves in a mirror. Rather than showing the person's real face, it's a virtual appearance that Yee can control, and then see the results as they 'meet' another person in a virtual world.

In one experiment that recalled the 1977 research, Yee assigned volunteers virtual faces judged to be of either high or low attractiveness. They then 'met' another person who saw a neutral face. Results showed that, during conversation, the volunteers who thought they were attractive revealed much more about themselves. They also stood very much closer to the second person in the virtual room.

A second experiment played with the idea that height is associated with confidence. Using the same experimental set-up, volunteers were led to believe that they were either 10 centimetres taller or 10 centimetres shorter than the second person in the virtual room, who saw everyone the same height. Volunteers were asked to play a confidence game, in which the two people in the virtual room had to suggest ways to split a pot of money. If one person offered a split and the other agreed, they both got the money. If the proposal was rejected, neither got the cash.

And the results showed that those who believed themselves taller than the other person consistently offered an unfair split of the money in their own favour. More than that, the volunteers who thought themselves shorter, consistently accepted a lower proportion in the split.

This shows how significant things like height are in our online identities, according to Yee. 'Eventually, when we get more used to being in virtual worlds, these effects may wash out, but for now, it seems that everyone is still acutely aware of those magnified traits', he told me. For him, these findings validate the Proteus Effect, and confirm the absolutely central role he believes our avatars play in the way we behave online.

The Clothes We Wear

What else might affect how we behave? Clothes make the man according to Francis_7, who makes films and designs clothes in There. I was intrigued to find that he has a female alter ego. He soon explained, however, that this was just so that he could more easily design women's outfits. 'In virtual worlds like There, clothes make a statement', he explained. The world doesn't allow you to choose your height, and there are limited hairstyles to select from. 'With limited choices for modifying your body, people use clothes instead. There are a lot of political message t-shirts.'

For young people, the experience of creating and dressing their avatar can be very significant too, according to Nic Crowe. 'There's a great pleasure in a search for a unique identity. So the idea that you can customise your identity or your avatar is very powerful', he told me. 'And young people follow the same rituals as in real life – putting on their best clothes to meet virtually.'

Do clothes cause a class divide – those who buy lots of new outfits versus those who don't? 'In any world there are haves and have-nots', says Francis. 'There are the poor new people, but most can afford a pretty reasonable look quite easily.'

'I think most take the route of looking how they wished they could look in real life', says Chagall, another Thereian. Like reality, but improved. Does she think that it makes socialising easier that most people look attractive? 'Yes. But back when I started I was awkward looking, and there were a few cliques of "beautiful people" that tended to snub others that didn't dress as nicely. I'm not sure if they did it on purpose, or if they even realized they were doing it.'

And there is indeed scientific evidence that our clothes – at least in terms of their colour – influence our behaviour. At the University of Texas at Austin, Jorge Peña has been investigating how this may extend into virtual worlds. He's created a testing environment using the combat action game Star Wars Jedi Knight II, in which his volunteers can wear particular costumes and interact on-screen.

'We know that your own external appearance can affect not only how people behave towards you but how you behave yourself. We wanted to test whether the same thing happens online', Jorge told me. In a legal setting, and in sports, research has shown that people are perceived as more aggressive and behave more aggressively if they are wearing dark colours.

'In the first experiment we had avatars dressed in a white or black cloak', said Jorge. 'We tested their aggression by looking at their attitudes towards people who were breaking a social rule.' He knew that, in online games, players had a custom that nobody attacked bystanders, people not actively participating in the game. 'So the task we gave people was to judge someone who broke this social rule, and to see how willing they were to break the rule themselves.' The findings were clear: the black-clothed avatars were more likely to try to break the rule. The white-clothed avatars showed no such change.

Jorge also measured the level of cohesion in a group. 'One idea is that when you are acting aggressively you inhibit more prosocial behaviours. For instance, if you're wearing black perhaps you're less likely to get a good team spirit. And this is what they found – white-clothed avatars were more social, and focused on being useful members of a team.

White-clothed **avatars** were more social, and **focused** on being **useful members of a team**

'The main question is: what's going on?' says Jorge. 'Are people identifying with an avatar because they happen to like dressing in black or white? Or are they affected by something else? My main hypothesis is that we are seeing a priming effect in which you are raising some association learned unconsciously from stereotypes, fairy tales or the media.' The effect of always seeing baddies dressed in black is coming home to roost.

Peña did a second study, dressing some people's avatars as white-clad medical doctors. Others were dressed as Ku Klux Klan (KKK) members – in white too, but with a negative association. There was also a control group whose avatars were see-through (the powers of working in cyberspace, eh). 'We invited everyone to look at a virtual museum with two ambiguous pictures on display, and then to write a story about what they'd seen. And the main finding is that the stories by those in doctor avatars were affiliative, and very positive in comparison with the Ku Klux Klan group', Jorge told me. The control group were somewhere in the middle. 'So we interpreted this as showing that the doctors were primed to think positive thoughts. By contrast, the KKK avatars wrote aggressive stories dealing with vengeance. They saw the same pictures, but associations kicked in and changed how people described the objects.'

▟▟ The doctors were primed to think positive thoughts. By contrast, the KKK avatars wrote aggressive stories dealing with vengeance ▐▐

'We did a debriefing to check that people didn't know what we were really testing and behave as they thought we wanted them to', he says of both experiments. 'If this were so, they would have said "I should behave antisocially because I'm dressed as a member of the Ku Klux Klan" or "because I'm wearing black". But they thought we were playing a negotiation game, or tracking their movements. The cover story worked.'

Jorge Peña believes the theory of priming is the reason why people conform to the colour of their clothes. But Nick Yee isn't sure whether the visual priming is enough to explain what happens in cyberspace. 'I think it's more than the visual priming effect. There's something special about being *in* a different body, on top of just seeing it', he told me.

Peña agrees more research is needed: 'We need to look at how people are doing this on a daily basis. The avatar may have an effect on you that you're not aware of. We need a deepened understanding of when we do things we intend, and when they are unconscious.'

But he's sure that avatars have an effect on your behaviour. 'If we can see the effect of an avatar you *didn't* choose and it affected you, we can expect that when you choose a stereotype, or an evil character, then you'll see a bigger effect. You are investing your public persona into that avatar. So I would think the effect is going to be stronger.'

Virtual Trust

As well as affecting our own behaviour and attitudes, our on-screen appearance is crucial in how trustworthy we seem, research shows.

Experiments at the University of Connecticut examined how we judge whether or not an avatar, and thus the person it represents, is credible. Researchers created a range of computer-drawn images, including a typically female depiction of a girl with pigtails, a person not clearly male or female, and a very non-human beer bottle with a face. This gave them scale of androgyny (male or female-ness) and anthropomorphism (more or less human). These characters were assigned randomly to a group of volunteers who were then asked to chat online in pairs – able to see their partner's avatar but not their own.

After 20 minutes, the volunteers rated whether they found their chat-partner trustworthy, and also how androgynous their avatar seemed. In a second experiment, different volunteers looked at the avatars and made snap decisions about trustworthiness and androgyny. The results were interesting. Participants' ratings of the avatars showed that those perceived as more masculine or feminine (the less androgynous), were perceived as more anthropomorphic. And the avatars that seemed more human also seemed more credible (you knew you couldn't trust that beer bottle).

Those **perceived** as **more masculine** or **feminine** (the **less** androgynous), were perceived as more **anthropomorphic**

'It is difficult to say how these results might transfer to true online communities', said Kristine Nowak, by email. 'Remember that these studies were done with people who had not interacted previously and did not expect to interact in the future.' But she was sure that there is a mapping from real-life behaviour to online worlds. 'I absolutely believe that the categories and communication processes we use offline – for example stereotypes – are transferring online, and research is consistent with that', she told me.

Are People Who They Seem to Be?

What if people deliberately play with their online persona? Nick Yee's research has shown that at any one time, half of the female characters in a MMO game are probably being played by men. Does this reveal a widespread psychological trait in male gamers?

At any one time, half of the female characters in a MMO game are probably being played by men

Well, probably not. The reasons men give for gender-swapping are generally quite practical. If they play a female character, that's the character they get the pleasure of looking at, sometimes for hours on end. They tend to get more attention and help from other players. 'Women are given more stuff by other players. So men think "it will increase my Uber-ness because people will feel sorry for me". Everyone knows people are gender bending', says Aleks Krotoski.

Only a very few women choose male characters: around one in a hundred, by Yee's research. Why don't they choose to try out a male avatar? Aleks explains: 'Women online tend to be idealized versions of their real selves. Men are much more interested in exploring facets: what if I had purple hair; what if I were a woman'.

Do you find these avatars trustworthy? Your avatar's appearance can alter how others perceive you online, according to Kristine Nowak's research. (There's also been some debate about whether the final image is a ketchup bottle or a beer bottle: what do you think?)

Experimentation is possible in an online world. 'I think it amplifies people's personalities', says Chagall, a Therian. 'In time people also experiment with other personalities. They make new avatars and act differently.' Theresa concurs: 'Second Life is a playground for adults', she says. 'You can fulfil fantasies safely there.'

A fantasy avatar that's just an experiment is one thing. What if someone's trying to influence you for more self-serving reasons? Well, there are all sorts of ways we can be influenced, even in a virtual setting, according to Nick Yee's findings.

Yee and colleague Jeremy Bailenson found that people were more strongly influenced by avatars that mimicked their own body movements. Seventy volunteers watching an avatar deliver a 3-minute speech found it much more convincing if the character copied their own head movements. Pre-programmed movements had no effect.

In another experiment on persuasion, Yee presented students with an image of an unfamiliar political candidate who he had morphed with a photograph of the

There is a fantasy world with environments that allow people to experiment.

students themselves. He found that when the student felt the face looked familiar, they were more likely to say they'd vote for the politician. And even when the morph contained 40% of the student's own face, fewer than 5% detected the trick. 'We were surprised at the low detection rates', says Yee. 'With less well-known candidates, some participants noted the candidate looked like someone they knew, a relative or friend.' But it sounds like most of us could easily fall victim to a cybercrime involving deception.

Gamecrime

Is there really any such thing as crime within a game? Surely not: the rules of a game are simply a social agreement. If you break them, surely it couldn't be classed as criminal activity? But strange and unpredictable things have always gone on in computer games. Here are five examples: racism, torture, bullying, cheating and boy-racing that show how games may be changing us or revealing something about the real world and ourselves in it.

Can Games Make You Racist?

For years there's been controversy surrounding the negative representation of ethnic minorities in computer games. There's now been heated debate over the portrayal of an ethnic *majority*: the fifth incarnation of zombie-blasting series Resident Evil seems to involve the white protagonist blowing away undead who are entirely black.

Along with a hackneyed view of the role and appearance of women, some games reveal their creators' twisted sense of what makes a fun activity – or limited brainpower for conceiving anything other than a stereotype.

But surely, in an online world where no one knows what you really look like, these factors wouldn't come into play? When I spoke to gamer Margaret Robertson, she gave a fascinating insight into the way that racial or geographic preconceptions may begin, grow and eventually turn into full-blown hatred. And it was all through her observations of life in the Massively Multiplayer online game World of Warcraft,

'In World of Warcraft, I play a giant cow called a Tauren, and I am part of the Horde. Taurens are in an uneasy truce with the orcs, trolls, the undead and the blood elves, so that we can fight the Alliance. The world is not dissimilar to ours, with an "American" continental lump and a "Eurasian" continental lump. The races of the Horde have learned each other's languages, but none of the Horde can speak the Alliance languages.

'Now, there are enormously involved backstories to the game and some people are obsessed by them. I have no idea why we are at war. But it doesn't mean I don't care. This inability to communicate is one of the most profound things I've experienced in a game. It generates hostility and suspicion. I now understand whole chunks of human history much better. Everything about your behaviour seems weird. I've wandered into Alliance territory and I've got distracted, stopped to go through my pockets or something – I'm just standing there. But then I look up and see two Alliance have stopped. You look automatically threatening; completely innocent gestures look aggressive.

'The Horde look like the bad guys: for some their jaws have rotted off, their tongues flap around. Orcs are ugly green lumps. Trolls have blue skin and huge tusks. The Alliance characters are prettier and more conventional than the Horde; they have fantasy-adventure looking people. Avuncular dwarfs who look like they should be chopping down trees. A tiny 18-inch-tall race, cute, with pink hair in bunches. Then there are the night elves and goddesses. They all live in beautiful dangly forests.

'I find fighting in the battles very stressful. But when I do fight, I find I have developed a hatred of the other races. Not because of any history, but because they seem stupid and silly and flouncy, and they are rubbish at capture-the-flag. You kind of want to kill them. I feel a real sense of belonging and protection to my homeland, not because I understand why we are there, but because that's where I started to play the game. It is a repository of my previous experiences and the memories of the people who helped me. I now love my homeworld.'

❮❮ When I do fight, **I find I have** developed a **hatred of the other races**. **Not because of** any **history,** but because they seem **stupid** and **silly** and **flouncy,** and they are **rubbish** at **capture-the-flag**. You **kind of want to kill them ❯❯**

Digital Nasties

Would you torture a fellow human being? You'd probably like to think you're above such things. But what about a virtual person? Does the word 'torture' mean anything when talking about zeros and ones instead of flesh and bone?

Torture: the word is certainly being bandied about a lot in relation to the strategic life-simulation game The Sims. This hugely popular game invites you to create and nurture virtual people – an animated and almost-sentient version of a doll's house. Sims, as the game characters are known, have needs. You can't just let them sit around – the aim of the game is to satisfy their basic requirements for food, company, work and toilet visits. If you don't, or you fail to monitor their every move, things can go wrong and they'll meet a sticky end or simply waste away. But rather than fostering the welfare of the characters they have created, some players prefer to see just how awful they can make their charges' lives.

'I burn them, trap them in a room while having a party then set everything on fire and watch them burn till they die', writes one Sim-killer. Others report building a swimming pool, allowing their Sims to get in and then deleting the steps so that the exhausted characters eventually drown. Or removing the fridge so that one or more Sims die of starvation – it only takes a couple of days. The interactions between Sims offer further possibilities for actual or social death: deleting all the toilets so that Sims die in a puddle of their own urine, or putting the house's only facilities in the living room so that Sims have to shamefully pee in front of each other. Apparently, it's all part of life's rich pattern.

Even 13-year-old girls, questioned about their reasons for liking The Sims, said that power was one of the big draws. 'I could control whatever they did – I could make their lives enjoyable or miserable', said one. 'I was in charge', said another. This fascination outweighed any other reason for wanting to play.

On messageboards relating to The Sims, nobody really seems very concerned about this behaviour. It's just another aspect of the game that players explore when they're bored with trying to improve their characters' lives: after all, satisfying a Sim's desire for a zebra-print sofa does sound a rather hollow achievement. It helps relieve the monotony to find out what happens along the other direction of the continuum – what happens if you actively try to make Sims' lives tragic?

What seems even more psychologically significant is when a player decides to kill a Sim in response to a real-life slight: 'Whenever someone really, really, seriously pisses me off, I'll create a Sim that looks like them, and I'll put them in one of those Sims Torture Houses', writes a 32-year-old female blogger from South Carolina. 'You build a small house, like maybe 3 × 3 tiles, no doors or windows.

And then you give them one of the most uncomfortable chairs and a sink. So all they can do is drink water or sit (though if they get tired enough, they'll sleep on the floor in pools of their own urine). This usually ends up with them (a) going mad, and (b) peeing themselves to death. Yes, I said peeing themselves to death. Also a couple of times that I did this, all the neighbours who came over to visit also went mad and peed themselves to death.' Nice.

▐▐ Whenever someone really, **really, seriously** pisses me **off,** I'll **create a Sim** that looks like **them,** and I'll **put** them in **one of those** Sims Torture Houses **▐▐**

If Sims are like dolls, there's probably little that's different between this behaviour and, say, playing toy soldiers. This is how Jon Sykes sees it – a psychologist and computer-games lecturer at Glasgow Caledonian University. 'Games allow us to play with demons', he explains. 'Lots of games and films deal with war: the play-world gives us the power to beat the terrorists. Games offer ways of exploring and playing about with concepts we find hard to deal with in real life.'

What if, on a **psychological** level, that **pixellated prostitute** is **real**?

But what about the fact that, given the choice to nurture or harm, so many Sims players choose the dark side? Sykes doesn't buy it as a form of 'real' torture. 'We don't really want to torture anyone – it's much more to do with reflecting our inner concerns', he says. It's also perhaps a way of working out the limits of the system the game puts in place. 'In Grand Theft Auto, you increase your stamina by having sex with a prostitute and then beating her up to get your money back. Now, watching over someone's shoulder I've been quite horrified by that. But to the player it's a task you have to complete; a mechanism to get to the next stage.'

What if, on a psychological level, that pixellated prostitute is real? Would we feel differently about the Sim-killers if science showed we thought of virtual characters were alive? New experiments are shedding light on this question.

The Shocking Science of Submission

Remember that classic 1960s experiment, when volunteers were invited to give a hidden victim increasingly strong electric shocks if they got the answers to questions wrong? Psychologist Stanley Milgram was trying to find out how far people would go in hurting another person if they thought they had been told to do so by an authority figure. In reality, there was no victim, just an actor, who begged for the electric shocks to stop with increasing desperation. Milgram found (against expectations that only a sadistic few would give the top-whack shock) that 65% of volunteers went all the way and administered a jolt that was apparently lethal.

It's considered an extremely revealing, but somewhat unethical experiment today. So what happens if you re-run the test using a virtual victim, represented like a game avatar? Scientists based at King's College London decided to see how participants would respond if asked to give a virtual character electric shocks in an immersive computer-generated environment. But they weren't interested in obedience, as Milgram sought to explore in the original experiment. No, their objective was to find out whether participants would respond as if this highly charged situation were real, even though they knew that it wasn't.

Here's the shocker: despite the fact that all participants knew for sure that neither the victim, nor the jolts, nor the victim's increasing protests were real, they tended to have strong emotional reactions. Skin conductance monitoring showed participants were aroused, while their electrocardiogram analysis showed stress as they shocked their obviously virtual victim. Some participants walked out of the test before it was complete. The scientists saw many volunteers try to help the victim avoid shocks by emphasising the right answers in the way they asked questions.

The researchers also checked on the significance of being able to see the victim, by testing some subjects in the immersive virtual environment, while others communicated just through a text interface with no audio feed. It's important whether you can see and hear your victim, it seems – people who tried the text version seemed to feel much less empathy with her.

Empathy, caring behaviour, clue-giving, seeking to save the virtual victim from pain . . . these results demonstrate how we see virtual people: they're *real* to us on some level.

Empathy, **caring behaviour**, clue-giving, **seeking to save the virtual victim** from **pain** . . . these results demonstrate **how we see** virtual **people**: they're **real** to us **on some level**

If VR environments do indeed provoke the same kind of response from volunteers as real life experiments with real people, they could help with a number of knotty psychological problems. Why, for example, do people become *less* likely to help someone being attacked in the street, the more bystanders there are? Maybe VR will provide a way to find out.

VR experiments have also provided evidence that we think virtual people are thinking. Among a small group of people who took part in a virtual experiment with computer-generated people, several responded positively to their virtual companions. But despite the neutral design of these pixel-people, a number of the real people developed a sense that the virtual characters were out to get them. It's clear – we're wired to believe that our computer-generated companions have feelings and consciousness. Looks like the Sim-killers may have some explaining to do, after all.

Bullying

Could a computer game do any good in helping to combat bullying? Cyberbullying is intimidation that takes place within games, in chat rooms, or even by mobile phone. It's not just happening among children: in the virtual world Second Life, hundreds of abuse reports are filed every day by adults reporting problems with other adults. The ubiquity of technology and its anonymity make cyberbullying hard to escape and tricky to root out. It also makes bizarre forms of attack possible: Second Life has in the past been troubled by antisocial plagues of flying penises that have pursued individuals or disrupted meetings.

Second Life has in the **past** been **troubled** by **antisocial** plagues of **flying penises**

The game Bully generated much publicity on launch – it was developed by Rockstar, the company that brought us Grand Theft Auto and Manhunt. But the more thoughtful critics saw it wasn't about glorifying violence, as the pre-launch debate had predicted. As you play the 'troubled schoolboy' at the centre of the game, you're not in the role of a bully at all, but involved in figuring out cunning ways to

Bully or victim? Games may help one understand the other.

beat them. Bully doesn't gloss over the daily anarchy of school life, and it doesn't offer any trite solutions. But it could provide a credible basis on which to discuss the problems.

You're **not** in the **role of a bully** at all, but **involved** in figuring out **cunning ways** to beat **them**

At a more experimental level, Fearnot! is a role-playing scenario game, developed by a group of European researchers. Players watch an animated sequence relating to bullying, and then type in suggested advice that influences the unfolding action. The system uses an emergent narrative system, weaving together input suggestions with existing character profiles. 'You're the character's invisible friend and you can influence him and try to help', explained the project's leader, Ruth Aylett from Heriot-Watt University in Edinburgh. The system is being trialled in the UK and Germany with children aged 8–12.

Driven to Distraction?

'He was a very nice person; very, very kind and very down to earth, a humble guy.' So said a colleague of Tahir Khan, a 46-year-old taxi driver in the Canadian city of Toronto. Khan was killed in January 2006 when a Mercedes-Benz hit his cab and slammed it into a streetlight. Police told journalists that the Mercedes was one of two cars racing at up to 140 kilometres per hour through the Toronto suburb, driven by 18-year-old former classmates. On the front seat of one of the speeding cars, investigators found a copy of Need for Speed, which simulates high-speed street racing. The two drivers, who had borrowed the high-powered cars from their parents, were arrested and charged with criminal negligence causing death.

Toronto Police said they believed the boys had been playing the game before they went out driving. 'Ninety-nine percent of the gamers understand it is just a game and not real life where you can press a button and hit re-set if you crash', said detective Paul Lobsinger. 'Here we have, in real life, two guys driving high-end cars at a high rate of speed in an urban area' – similar to the way the game is played, he alleged in an interview with Canada's 24 Hour News service.

Is this another media myth – a case in which a computer game is again in the frame when something goes tragically wrong? Or is it true that a computer game can make you into a boy racer?

Car-racing games have been a popular genre for years: some of the earliest games involved guiding a 2-D top-down 'car' from side to side while the 'road' scrolled down the screen. But today's racing games are a different animal all together. As Steven Poole points out in his book about game aesthetics, *Trigger Happy*, 'In the racing game, graphics and speed are part of the "feel". Every increase in [games machines'] technological power enhances the genre's unique pleasure: the feeling of hurtling a vehicle around a realistic environment at suicidal velocities.'

One brand of racing game is very realistic in nature: the serious kind of simulation in which players drive a Formula One styled car around Grand Prix circuits, picking real 'driving lines', accelerating and braking skillfully for success. But many racing games allow players to drive in ways they never would in reality, in locations that they never could – the Japanese suburbs in Gran Turismo or the urban environment similar to New York or Los Angeles in Need for Speed: Underground.

And for Poole, this second category is what racing games are really all about. If you can't practise 'amusingly dangerous and unlikely manoeuvres' in a racing title, why call it a game at all? The chance to challenge your friends adds to the thrill: 'the perfect opportunity for competitive two-person action'.

Do computer games make your driving worse?

But what effect might this be having on drivers' real behaviour? Could Need for Speed really lead drivers to take the ultimate chance on a suburban road? René Weber is an Assistant Professor of Mass Communication at the University of California Santa Barbara, USA. He says that there is still a distinction between reality and virtuality. 'The argument is that once you are exposed to a real threat – so that one result of what you do is that you might die – that changes your behaviour since survival-relevant stimuli become relevant', he told me. 'Simulated driving and real driving may feel very different.' In other words, you don't drive at the 'suicidal velocities' of a game on the real road because you know the possibility exists of real-life death.

Cruisin' for a Bruisin'

But new research suggests that some people may be ignoring that risk. Peter Fischer, a psychologist at Munich's Ludwig-Maximilians University, reported research in 2006 that suggests racing games can provoke unsafe driving. Fischer and his team interviewed 290 randomly selected drivers whom they found at petrol stations and fast-food restaurants. Those who reported playing more computer racing games also tended to have the most aggressive driving habits.

27% admitted they thought they took **more risks** after **gaming sessions**. A similar number – **mainly men** – said **they imagine themselves** in a **driving game** while **they are on the real roads**

The 198 men and 92 women in Fischer's research had an average age of 23 – within the 17–25 range at which accidents are more likely. Under-24s were also the focus of a 2007 survey by a UK driving instruction company British School of Motoring. They asked 1000 young drivers about their driving and gaming habits, finding that more than a third said they were more likely to drive faster after playing on-screen driving games. Twenty-seven percent admitted they thought they took more risks after gaming sessions. A similar number – mainly men – said they imagine themselves in a driving game while they are on the real roads.

Why Are Young Men Bad Drivers?

Could racing games be feeding into a culture of driving bravado, in which on-screen activity supports a desire to show that one is a talented, experienced driver?

- UK statistics show that young drivers are up to 10 times more likely to be killed or injured than more experienced drivers.
- Young drivers account for 27% of driver fatalities while making up only 10% of the population across the USA, EU, Australia, Japan and South Korea.
- One insightful report showed that over-confidence was one of the main problems. 'Drivers who are high in confidence . . . lack caution and have a tendency to take on challenges that are beyond their capabilities', it found.
- Evidence shows that driving can be a way of expressing identity – especially for young men. To project confidence behind the wheel is therefore a mechanism for positioning oneself as an experienced, in-control driver, even if the facts show otherwise.
- If there are passengers in the car, the research found, a driver often feels the need to show off.
- Young men are far more likely than others to indulge in competitive driving on the road.

If driving is all about self-image, an interviewee is likely to choose survey responses that bolster a swaggering attitude towards driving.

At the University of Munich, Peter Fischer followed up his interview-based study with more research. The team asked 83 male students at Ludwig-Maximilians University to play a computer game for 20 minutes – either a street-racing game (Burnout, Midnight Racer or Need for Speed) or one unrelated to cars and driving (platform game Crash Bandicoot or football game FIFA 2005). To succeed in the racing games, players had to 'massively violate traffic rules', according to the researchers, driving on the pavement, crashing deliberately into other vehicles, and – inevitably – driving at high speed. Immediately after playing the games, participants did a word quiz, giving the definition of a list of words with two possible meanings – one risk-related and one not. For example, the German word *rasen* means either 'lawn' or 'to drive at high speed'; while the word *trauen* means either 'to get married' or 'to dare to do something'. Results showed that racing-game players were more likely to come up with the risky word than the safe-sounding version: a result that showed that risk-related thoughts had come to the forefront of their minds.

Fischer's team took a third approach to the question of whether game-risk equals driving-risk. Sixty-eight drivers aged 19–35 played either a computer racing game, or a game unrelated to driving. The researchers then showed them a series of video-based driving scenarios, and asked participants to indicate what action they would take if they were driving. These scenarios are routinely used in Germany to test whether banned drivers should get their licences back. Surprise, surprise, in Fischer's experiment, volunteers who had just played the racing game took their chances – they selected options involving shooting the level-crossing barrier as it started to close, or overtaking another driver in a risky situation.

Surprise, surprise. I'm serious. There's been very little previous research linking driving games to risky road-driving. But the fact is that it's highly possible that young drivers have spent many more hours practising in a virtual car than a real one. The British School of Motoring survey found that more than a third of the 1000 drivers questioned thought that driving games could actually improve real-life driving ability and encourage faster reflexes.

It's **highly** possible that **young drivers** have spent **many more hours practising** in a **virtual car than a real one**. The BSM survey found that more than a **third** of the **1000** drivers **questioned** thought that driving games could **actually** improve **real-life** driving ability and **encourage faster** reflexes

Games researcher James Newman points out that driving games rarely teach you anything about driving that you can apply in real life. 'All but the most casual of players learns that "bouncing" off the scenery and, especially, careering into other vehicles is an extremely effective means of taking tight corners', he says in his book *Videogames*. 'Certainly, it is easier than trying to pick a racing line.'

Could this 'try it and see' approach be one that game-playing young drivers try to apply in real life? The DfT research found evidence that post-test drivers *expect* to experience accidents as part of their learning process: 'There is a widespread fatalism about the inevitability of accidents', the authors stated.

Peter Fischer and his team can't specifically say what the mechanism might be to explain their results linking gaming and riskier driving. By playing a risky game, players may be reinforcing cognitive pathways relating to risky behaviour – plus positive messages about risk-taking – that they then apply elsewhere. But there are other possible explanations. People who play racing games experience a range of frustrating events when they're overtaken or rammed as part of the game. Perhaps this makes them more used to feeling frustrated when they drive for real, an emotion often linked with aggression in psychological theory. Or maybe gaming desensitises players to risky road situations. Fischer also notes that he can't tell whether or not the immediate effects of gaming seen in the study have a long-term impact.

Whatever the mechanism, gamers young and old have claimed an effect on real-life driving from playing racing games. One New York State driver, chased for almost an hour across two counties by police trying to enforce his parole order, claimed he thought he could outrun his pursuers because of the skills he'd gained playing Grand Theft Auto. He was eventually sent to prison for 7 years for assault.

At the other end of the spectrum, at least one respectable 65-year-old is feeling the same effects. 'My dad loves car racing games', Alun Ward, a graphic designer and game tutor, told me. 'It does make him put his foot down at roundabouts. He sets the game to "no damage" and he sometimes seems to be looking for a button on the dashboard to do the same.'

He sets the **game** to **"no damage"** and he **sometimes** seems to be looking for a **button on the dashboard** to do the **same**

One *New Scientist* forum post admitted: 'I have Burnout 4, which is racing pretty much based on aggressive driving. I've learnt not to play half an hour or so before driving, cause it's a bit distracting to have those images floating around.'

Tom, 36, said 'I remember spending a whole evening playing the first Grand Theft Auto and thinking it was really funny. Then the next morning I woke up and found out that someone had been playing it for real here in my town – or rather, that they had stolen a pick-up truck and killed two policemen. It wasn't quite so funny after that. Of course the link was just in my mind.'

Rekha, 24, said she'd enjoyed Need for Speed: Carbon so much that she'd bought a driving wheel with pedals to use with the game. Any ill effects? She admitted 'wanting to drive fast in driving lessons.'

But René Weber has no qualms about playing racing games himself. 'I'm a fan of playing racing games to relax. You can play them quickly – if I've got 20 minutes I can play a race, get excited and have fun.'

Some people in my survey knew it was just a game. 'I soon realised that I couldn't drive my car that fast around town like on the game using buttons and toggles', said Simon, 37. One respondent wrote over 400 words explaining how much he enjoyed the gameplay and competition of street-racer Speed Buster without ever referring to a real-life experience.

And just to make any conclusions about screen and real-life driving even less clear, research at the University of Rochester has concluded – you guessed it – that gamers drive *better* than non-gamers. It's known that safe driving is not strongly correlated with having good eyesight, but with an ability to monitor a cluttered visual world seen through the windscreen. So researchers used a test that measured people's abilities to spot a target flashed on a screen for just 7 milliseconds. Even when the cunning scientists added squares to the display to distract viewers, the computer-game players in the sample far outperformed the non-gamers.

Cheating

Can you cheat at a computer game? The questionable morality of all the available *cheats* for succeeding in some games led researcher Mia Consalvo to publish a book in 2007. She examined more closely than ever before the practice of using special codes for 'God mode' in which you can't be killed; swapping clues or entire walkthroughs of games on the Internet, or the programmer-types who can crack the whole thing open and see how it works.

Consalvo found three mentalities: the purists who never would, the pragmatists who'll use cheats as a last resort, and the compulsive cheaters who just use any means necessary to get to the end. Where do you sit on the continuum? You might never try to beat an opponent with unfair tactics. But what about a single-player game? Hear Gareth's salutary tale about the puzzle game Starship Titanic:

'Early on in the game, I thought I might have found a bug. Logically, I thought I'd solved a puzzle, but a bit of the screen wasn't behaving as I expected and I couldn't get anywhere. It was early enough in the game that I didn't mind starting again if necessary, but I wanted to make sure that I wasn't barking up the wrong tree before I threw away my progress so far.

'So I found a walkthrough on the Internet, downloaded it and read up to the point that I was stuck on. And I was right – I'd done exactly what the walkthrough said, and the game wasn't responding as it should. So I deleted my saved game and started again, and it didn't take me long to get back to the point I was at. At that point, I really should have deleted the walkthrough from my hard drive, because it was a little bit too accessible. Every time I was just a little bit stuck, I'd find myself cheating so that I could move on to the next bit. The result was that I finished the game in a weekend, and it didn't feel like an achievement – it felt like a waste of 40 quid. And I learned the valuable lesson that you're only cheating yourself.'

❝ I learned the **valuable lesson** that **you're only cheating yourself** ❞

Conclusion

How do we know who we are – and who others are – when playing a game? The research shows that we transfer our real-world faculties into cyberspace in order to judge each other's personality and behaviour – as well as making decisions about our own. But we don't stop there. We also show a propensity to assign real human significance to computer-generated virtual characters. We might soon have to consider the possibility that, even in cyberspace, we're our brothers' keepers.

We might soon have to **consider the possibility** that, even in **cyberspace,** we're our **brothers' keepers**

Despite appearances to the contrary, moral and ethical codes are alive and well in the world of computer games. Gamecrime may not always operate as we expect – and we may not always be acting consciously. But in the examples we've seen, it's clear that our sensibilities about right and wrong extend into the virtual realm.

If the game-world is one where our behaviour actually *matters*, then what we do there is all the more significant. Despite the role-play, the fantasy and the suspension of disbelief, somehow it's still us there, on the screen, doing our thing. It may sound as though we are limiting ourselves simply because we can't conceive of a world where we or others are any different to reality. But on the contrary, by remaining true to ourselves when we play, computer games become a powerful tool by which we can know ourselves and explore the limits of what we can really do.

4 Can Computer Games Turn You into an Addict?

Introduction

'**EverQuest was one of the** primary reasons my fiancé's first marriage broke up', Amanda, 30, tells me. 'He says now that the game was like a full time job, he played upwards of 50 hours each week – putting the game before all else (including his wife and two children). After his wife left him, he deleted the game from his computer, destroyed the software and didn't play for 6 months. After 6 months he started playing again with a vow to himself that he would never go back to the way he was and that he would never again let the game ruin a relationship.

'When I met him he had started playing again, a minimum of 4 hours every night. Knowing his history, I was scared, but I let him talk me into an agreement – he would only play one night a week (Saturday) for a maximum of 4 hours. Things seemed to be going fine until I discovered he was playing outside of the agreed-upon day. His children (who he only sees every other weekend) started

Are computer games as addictive as any other vice?

PHOTOGRAPH BY IVAN MELENCHON SERRANO

PHOTOGRAPH BY MICHELLE KWAJAFA

complaining to me that daddy was spending all day playing "his old game". I felt betrayed.'

Amanda is at a crossroads. She needs to make a decision: has her fiancé really changed? Is he right to say she should trust him not to go back to his 50-hour-a-week habit? Should she compromise to save her relationship – after all, she occasionally enjoys computer games, too? Or will that ultimately lead to a path of destruction for her forthcoming marriage?

'Now it is a constant battle because he thinks I am being unreasonable and I think he should stick to the agreement we originally had', says Amanda. 'We generally have a very good relationship but now I am feeling paranoid'.

If you've not heard a story like Amanda's before, it probably sounds like a rare case of excessive game-playing. It's sad for Amanda, of course, but most grown men would be able to tell the difference between playing a game for fun and risking the destruction of a second relationship.

❝ I get full of rage when I see him **sitting** there **wasting away** in front of that **computer**. He is **missing out on time** he could **spend with us**, his **flesh and bone** family **❞**

And it's true, you don't meet people like Amanda very often. But she and thousands of others like her are reaching out across the Internet to share their experiences of partners, friends and children who don't seem to be able to stop playing computer games. Obsessive gamers are giving their own testimonies, first-hand accounts of how they somehow became dependent on a game – often with devastating results.

Some of these stories are heart-rending, as these anonymous quotes taken from websites for obsessive gaming illustrate:

'I have been married for 6 years and my husband has been playing this whole time. I am depressed and on medications. I feel lonely and tired all the time. I have a 10-yr-old daughter from before we met and I have a 2-yr-old boy between us. He pays attention when it's convenient and tells me what I'm doing wrong, but will not help.'

'My husband figured it out sooner than I that this game was becoming a problem. So he tried to

work on our marriage as I was still sitting behind the screen trying to avoid my problems and play with my "friends".'

'About a year ago I was addicted to video games, I played an online game called Halo 2 all day and night. During this time I had horrible grades. I didn't care about anything besides the game.'

'My life feels empty and I admit I get full of rage when I see him sitting there wasting away in front of that computer. He is missing out on time he could spend with us, his flesh and bone family, his family with needs and feelings.'

How can a game become more important to people than their 'flesh and bone' family? Why can't they break free from the screen and return to real life?

Games have always been an all-consuming experience for some people. Excessive gaming can affect men, women, teenagers and even relatively young children; married, single, at school, at college; all night, all day, all weekend. And now, online game worlds like EverQuest, World of Warcraft and RuneScape offer endless experiences – a game without end – and an infinite sequence of rewards for those prepared to put in the time to acquire them.

So why are some people affected by addiction while others shrug the experience off as 'just a game'? What's the science and psychology behind obsessive gaming? Are online games any more addictive than those on your computer desktop or console? And what are the signs and symptoms of problem gaming that you can look out for?

Why Are Games So Compelling? There's a Biological Reason

In a ground-breaking experiment in 1998, scientists invited a group of gamers to play a tank-battle action game while undergoing a brain scan. The type of scan, positron emission tomography (PET), involves injecting a radioactive tracer into the body and then tracking it to produce a three-dimensional 'map' of what's going on within.

In this case, the scientists used a radioactive tracer selected for its ability to show whether dopamine was being produced in the subjects' brains. This natural brain chemical plays a role in a wide range of behaviour, helping to reinforce things we find pleasurable. The eight men who had agreed to participate in the study had their brains scanned using the tracer while playing the tank game, which involved driving their tank to collect flags as rewards. On a different day, they had a second scan while simply staring at a blank screen, so as to establish their normal dopamine levels.

As they expected, the researchers saw a spike in dopamine levels when the gamer successfully captured a flag – up to double in some areas. The activity appeared in the brain areas connected with reward and learning. What was rather shocking, however, was the level of dopamine released during gameplay – equivalent, the researchers stated, to an intravenous injection of amphetamines or a dose of Ritalin.

It was the first time that scientists had managed to 'see' the brain's dopamine response to a particular behaviour. And was it a possible mechanism for understanding why computer games are addictive for some people?

The level of dopamine released during gameplay is equivalent, the researchers stated, to an intravenous injection of amphetamines or a dose of Ritalin

It certainly seems possible. Once the brain has been bathed in pleasurable chemicals, it seeks to repeat the experience. The trouble is that it eventually gets accustomed to the 'hit' and starts needing a bigger and bigger flood to gain satisfaction.

Other research at the Charité University Medicine Berlin examined the brain's response to gaming in a different way. Scientists tested two groups of 15 men, in their twenties – one group self-confessed game junkies and as a control group, game-players who weren't obsessed. They showed the two groups a series of images in which some were neutral, like chairs, and others were potentially provocative, such as alcohol-related images and screenshots of the men's favourite games. The non-game images provoked no unusual reactions, even though all the men enjoyed alcohol. But measurements of electrical activity in the volunteers' brains showed that the hard-core gamers were significantly more stimulated when exposed to computer game-related imagery than the ordinary gamers.

Were the excessive gamers really addicted? Or was there another explanation? It's possible that the extra brain activity was due to the gamers' ability to *read* the game images, extracting information that the neutral images did not contain. The similarity between the brain's learning and reward processes would make it hard to distinguish two phenomena with similar results.

But a further experiment lent weight to the addiction theory. The researchers also tested the avid gamers' reaction to screenshots from their favourite games. The group showed classic signs of craving: they desperately wanted to play the games, planned to do so, and expected the play to give them satisfaction. To the scientists, this demonstrated that they had learned a response to the game imagery in a similar way that visual cues can send a drug addict searching for another fix – even if he or she has been clean for months.

They had **learned** a response to the **game imagery** in a similar way that visual cues can **send a drug addict searching** for **another fix**

This evidence that the obsessive players had become reliant on the games for their 'high' is what the researchers believe proved they were addicted. By using only one coping strategy for life's problems – in this case, gaming – that became the only activity which could provide the dopamine buzz the addicts sought. 'It's the same mechanism in all addicts', said Sabine Grusser, who led the project.

It's What You Do, and the Way That You Do It

So for some players, games may provide an irresistible dose of brain-drugs that they come to rely on. But that's not the only way to understand why some become game-obsessed. Other researchers look to other behavioural addictions to explain computer-game compulsion. Professor Mark Griffiths at Nottingham Trent University is an expert in addictions including slot machines, bingo and computer games. He argues that all excessive behaviours have certain things in common, whether they involve ingesting a substance or twiddling a joystick.

Griffiths is keen to say that in his experience, true addiction to computer-game playing is relatively rare. 'I've come across very few true addicts, in the way that people are addicted to alcohol or drugs', he told me. Nonetheless, he says 'it's quite clear that any activity that takes over your life can have a negative effect.' Even at a level below addiction, excessive gaming can certainly cause problems. But how do you define 'excessive'?

For Professor Griffiths, it's all to do with context. 'You can have two people exhibiting exactly the same behaviour, and for one it's a problem and the other it isn't', he points out. 'I've seen a case where a 21-year-old was playing EverQuest for 16 hours a day. There was no detriment to his life because he had no partner and no children. When he did get a job or a partner, he just cut back on playing the game. But if you have a 38-year-old guy with three kids playing 16 hours a day, you'd probably find your wife would leave you.'

The idea that computers could be addictive was suggested long before Internet access made online worlds like EverQuest widely available. Nottingham University academic Margaret Shotton carried out a study back in 1989, investigating the characters and experiences of 127 children and adults who felt themselves to be 'hooked' on computer games. She found the majority were intelligent, motivated and achieving people, but tended to feel misunderstood. Shotton followed up 5 years later, and among the younger group, most had done well educationally, gone to university and then into good jobs. But all tended to prefer solitary hobbies and would have happily continued building their own car in the garage, making telescopes, pursuing photography or composing music. The study found no particular disadvantages to this alternative hobby of 'gaming'.

Shotton's book was entitled *Computer Addiction?* and for many experts, the question mark is still needed. Jerald Block is a psychiatrist with a particular interest in the impact of computers on people's mental lives. He has also seen many cases of computer over-use – but doesn't call it addiction. 'A lot of people use the word addiction, but psychiatrists don't like it because it's emotionally packed and carries different meanings', he told me from his office in Portland, Oregon. 'I use the term *pathological computer use*; we have pathological gambling, so there is a precedent. The other option is *compulsive computer use* where the person has a need to fulfil their habit on the computer'.

So, experts are still debating the right terminology. For some, the word *addiction* means specifically a need for a drug or alcohol. Others choose to describe these tendencies with the words *abuse* and *dependence*. Then again, the need to play computer games might be better termed an *obsession*, categorising it with straightforward behavioural problems.

Symptoms and Signs

Whatever the official definition, how can you tell if playing games is becoming a problem for you? A handful of high-profile cases in which game addiction has been blamed for self-harm or neglect of others means that this is becoming quite a loaded question. Most people who play games don't develop a harmful obsession with them. But the truth is that gaming is extremely compelling, even for 'normal' players.

❝ The principle of addiction is that you're playing against your better judgement; it's detrimental to other aspects of life ❞

'The principle of addiction is that you're playing against your better judgement; it's detrimental to other aspects of life', says Margaret Robertson, who as well as being a gamer is also a former editor of respected games magazine *Edge*. 'Dedicated gamers have mostly had times when this is true: staying up too late, or getting up too early, just to play the game. And I certainly know I've been late for things because I was gaming.'

It's exactly the aspects of games that make them engaging that can also lead to problems. Games offer the validation of reward – an interactive facet that's lacking in other media. They are often structured around a series of challenges to tackle and puzzles to solve – strings of achievements to celebrate. But for some, the desire to repeat their success makes them oblivious to anything other than the buzz.

What's Addiction All About? Expert Mark Griffiths Gives His Definitions

Salience – is playing computer games the most important thing in your life? If it dominates your thoughts, feelings and actions it has gained salience.

'When [Final Fantasy 7] first came out, my boyfriend and I took turns playing and ended up playing for pretty much three days straight. We hadn't realized that two extra nights had passed and felt absolutely horrible physically afterwards.' Female, 23, quoted in research by Mark Griffiths.

Mood modification – do you get a huge buzz out of playing games? Or do you feel a tranquillising sense of escape? These could both be signs you're using games to cope with some other problem.

'The BattleNet enabled the player to play the same game with up to 8 players over the Internet, this was really important to keep me motivated, I played it with friends for more than 3 years, sometimes more then 24 hours at the weekend. During school I played it 3–7 hours a day.' Felix, 19, Diablo II: Lord of Destruction fantasy action game player

'I still can't complete the 4 card game in the time allowed of ten minutes and find it really frustrating and addictive.' Sarah, 43, Spider Solitaire player

Tolerance – do you need more and more gameplay to achieve the enhanced mood you're after?

'As with any challenging game, you'll tend to feel angry when you lose. But unlike other games, instead of quitting the game in rage, I just launched another game.' Damien, 23, Speed Buster player

Withdrawal symptoms – the shakes, moodiness and irritability: all signs of withdrawal when you're separated from the game.

'Video games are plenty addictive in themselves. I love playing more than anyone, however, when told to stop after what I considered to be an unfair time, I got angry. Long story short, there is a foot sized hole in my wall.' From a message posted to the Physorg website, 2007

Conflict – does your gameplay create conflict with people in 'real life'; does it take you away from other hobbies or work, and what about your own feelings of time wasted?

'Financially I spend too much sometimes. I also have had to regulate my time in the game so I pay attention to real life issues and priorities. I have to prioritize my time.' Aveena, 57, There player

Relapse – have you ever given up your game, only to go back to it?

'I quit WoW about three months ago successfully. I pissed my wife off, neglected my new daughter, and got WAY behind on completing my graduate thesis. I'm nearing the end of my thesis now and am actually excited about the prospect of having time to play WoW again; I just don't know if I should, given that I've already kicked it.' – comment on WoW-detox.com

US media watchdog The National Institute on Media and the Family (NMIF) gives some top tips for spotting computer game obsession among children: spending most of non-school hours on the computer, falling asleep at school, performing unusually poorly academically, being irritable, lying about time spent gaming and choosing to game rather than see friends.

Clearly many of these symptoms might be due to other temporary obsessions – or just 'being an adolescent', when developing a sense of judgment seems to be achieved mainly by trial and error.

For adults, the list to watch according to the NMIF includes thinking about gaming all the time, spending time on games to the detriment of family, social and work life, lying about computer use, experiencing intense feelings of pleasure and guilt in relation to computer games, and a terrible sense of anger or depression when not playing a game.

A healthy enthusiasm will **add** something to your life, **whereas** an **addiction** is **taking away** from **your life**

More tangible issues could include overspending on games or online game access, not being able to sleep, physical aches and pains, dry eyes, a lack of proper nutrition or hygiene and good old carpal tunnel syndrome. Indeed, Mark Griffiths has done a comprehensive review of the research into negative effects of gaming, and can duly add to the pile of possibilities: numb toes or fingers, auditory hallucinations and seizures.

Griffiths points out that most people don't come away from playing a game with any of these symptoms. As he says: 'a healthy enthusiasm will add something to your life, whereas an addiction is taking away from your life.'

What Is the Impact of Excessive Game-Playing?

For those whom it strikes, game addiction is only too real. What's it like to be a computer-game addict? You can ask current and recovering problem players:

'I wasted a year and a half by not getting good results for my A levels.' Qi Wen, 21, World of Warcraft online questing game player

'I have never been this addicted to anything before. My other hobbies are gone. My daily blogging regimen has taken a hit. And my social life revolves more and more around friends in the game . . .' Entrepreneur Joi Ito writing about World of Warcraft in Wired, *2004*

'I started gaming seriously when I was at university in Beijing and got my first computer. I played endlessly, only stopping to sleep or eat. It affected my studies. I never went to class and I didn't even get to know my teachers. Gaming helps you avoid thinking about the problems of

life. Sometimes when you make friends in real life it is not as easy as when you are online, playing in one team . . . I have quit now because I wanted to be the centre of a real world.' Sylvia, interviewed for BBC Online, 2007

For others, the idea of obsession with a game is something light-hearted and unlikely to cause more than an occasional tiff with friends or family.

'If I hadn't discovered this game I would probably be much better at playing the guitar than I am. Personal problems are fine – in fact I had a girlfriend who would get up early to play, instead of staying in bed with me ; -)' Arran, 32, Civilization player

Some games require a time commitment for a player to succeed. Mark Griffiths speculates that devotees of the massively multiplayer online fantasy game Ever-Quest have to make sacrifices in their 'real' lives if they are to cope with the complexity of the game and the need to participate in group activities. In one of the earliest formal surveys of online game players, Griffiths surveyed 540 Ever-Quest players in 2004 to examine their demographics, motivation for playing, and whether they'd ever given anything up in order to devote time to the game. Just over a quarter said they sacrificed another hobby in order to play – fair enough. But nearly a fifth said they lost sleep in order to play, while others said they'd sometimes sacrificed time supposed to be spent on education, at work or with family to play.

Children – Dependent on Computer Games?

Parents often express concern about their children's obsession with games. One mother of a 6-year-old told me of her anxiety that her son played RuneScape at every available moment. He was allowed to play for a short while before school, and then again afterwards. But she felt it was affecting his behaviour, causing him to pick fights and snap at his siblings. On a week away from home and without access to the computer, 'he was sweetness and light.'

Reports of children addicted to games go back several decades. In one case a 13-year-old boy in Des Moines, Iowa, had developed such a habit of playing Pac-Man in the arcades that he became a serial burglar. For this boy, the benefits of fulfilling his brain's desire for reward – even the reward of 'eating' digital dots – outweighed the risk of his illegal activity. Other stories showed children spending school lunch money on games, or playing truant from school to spend time gaming.

Today, game-addiction may be a hidden and growing problem for the young. 'You see compulsive computer use in all ages', psychiatrist Jerald Block told me. 'But in the USA or UK, people don't usually find it a problem until they're older. Kids have more spare time, so they can fill their days with gaming and the fallout is not immediately noticeable – the games don't make people get into accidents or have alcoholic seizures. The repercussions can be hidden. However, when you look at Asian countries – places like Korea or China – the middle and high school years are very difficult and the students do not have much spare time. In these same countries, the physicians are seeing large numbers of kids who seem to be failing school because of their computer game use: in China, they estimate around 10 million such kids. In Korea, according to the Korean government, around 20% of adolescents are at risk.'

The Panorama Experience

A BBC Panorama investigation in 2007 looked at how families would cope without their usual fixes of games and television. Dubbed 'the longest TV deprivation study in the UK', the programme-makers arranged to remove all screen-based entertainment from half the families of a year three class in Manchester for 2 weeks. Scientific input to the project was from the director of the Centre for Mass Communication Research at Leicester University, Barrie Gunter.

According to the 2006/07 ChildWise Monitor Report, the average time that 5- to 16-year-olds watch television in the UK is currently 2 hours and 24 minutes daily. Before Panorama's ban, one pair of brothers watched around 3 hours of television every day: 'loads and loads and loads', as one of them put it. Sisters Natasha and Olivia had three televisions, including one to watch in their bedroom, supposedly to help them get to sleep. And James spent an hour and 20 minutes each day on his PlayStation Portable (PSP).

Addicted to screen entertainment? You might have thought so. But, deprived of TV and games, these 7- and 8-year-olds actually found it remarkably easy to fill their time. Traditional games like Buckaroo, Scrabble and Guess Who? were rediscovered and dusted off. Some of the children surprised themselves with what they didn't miss: 'I've been coping without the television very well', said one boy. 'On Saturday I'd be watching the telly for most of the day, and doing nothing really. I'm not that bothered really when we get our television back.' And the parents saw a real difference in family life. One mum said 'We did notice that when we didn't have the telly there was less arguing, less fighting.' More positive results emerged from another household: 'There was a lot more laughter in the house. We were having a good laugh and we kind of, you know, we were more of a family. It's really really odd.' James' mum told him 'You're just like your normal self again. It's nice to see you playing isn't it, and laughing and having fun, which you just don't do when you're on that PSP, do you?'

Mind you, this was only day 5 of the 14-day study. By the weekend, several parents were wishing for the screens' swift return to give them a break. 'The children are being very silly, which you just don't need first thing on a Sunday morning, do you really?' moaned one mum. 'This is the first time I actually want the TV, just to initiate some control.' Another parent admitted: 'It's definitely been a lot messier not having the telly. They are a lot more tired and to be honest I'm more tired as well.' As the programme's presenter put it 'Take away the television and mum and dad have to work harder.'

So who was the most dependent on games and TV? Initially, the focus was on how the children would cope without their usual fixes of screentime. But, ultimately, it was the parents who had to find ways to cope without the sedative effects of games and television. 'TV was being used in ways which I think the parents had not really thought about for quite some time', said Barrie Gunter. Without screen-based entertainment, 'members of the family then have to engage one another, they have to pay more attention and a different quality of attention to each other.' On the whole this was a positive thing. 'The kids felt they were getting more and better attention from mum and dad, and in many ways that calmed them down, because one of the reasons why kids often get excited is because they're attention-seeking.'

'Parents need to think what is best for their children, and try to turn them into rounded human beings', suggests Mark Griffiths, himself a father of three. And many children know at some level that life with the screen might not be healthy. My 5-year-old son, when asked what would happen if we let him watch television and play computer games all day, replied sagely 'I would get hungry.'

Time-Consuming Games Aren't Necessarily Harmful

Most games take ages. Now that I have two small children, I look back reverently on the years when I had time to play the game Myst, an exploration game in a series that could easily have taken up the rest of my life, had I only given it the chance. For some people, perhaps particularly younger players, this time-filling quality of computer games is actually quite useful. Rather than taking them away from more productive activities (bob-a-job wasn't exactly high up the agenda anyway), games soak up some of the time that might otherwise have been whiled away in less-than-social ways.

In any case, there's evidence that most school-age gamers somehow still find time to fit in their homework. Researchers at the University of Michigan studied the habits of nearly 1500 10- to 19-year-olds by tracking their activities on weekdays and weekend. Just over 500 of them played games regularly, about 80% of whom were boys.

I could easily have spent even more hours than I did playing the immersive game Myst.

They found that boys spent 58 minutes, on average, playing on a weekday, and 1 hour 37 minutes gaming on a weekend day. Girls spent 44 minutes playing on a weekday and an hour and 4 minutes on a weekend day. It certainly adds up: these figures would mean secondary school-age boys are playing games for the equivalent of two and a half weeks in a year. But did anything suffer as a result of the gaming? Hope Cummings says the findings were mixed: 'Gamers did spend less time reading and doing homework', she told *New Scientist*. 'But they didn't spend less time interacting with their parents or their friends, nor did they spend less time in sports or active leisure activities.'

Older gamers can find that games' time-gobbling effect isn't always as positive. 'There were weekends when I was playing the strategy game Civilization II and I'd be aware it was time for dinner', Greg, a 32-year-old gamer, told me. 'But the thing about these games is, just playing for another ten minutes is actually playing for an hour and a half. Game-wise it feels much shorter. You do set goals and you say "right as soon as I've just conquered that city, then I'll have a cup of tea or I'll have my breakfast. Or lunch". But instead of it taking ten minutes to knock off a city, it takes longer because you have to wait for resources to come in. It might have taken an hour and a half just to build up your army.'

And Margaret Robertson describes how 'time spent playing' some games can hide an essentially social experience. 'If I play World of Warcraft for three hours, I'll spend two hours playing and one hour in a field catching up with people; mucking around', she told me. 'I'm not really interacting with the game, I'm in a nice spot with a couple of friends trying to sit on a fence and look good for a photograph.'

Studies have found that game-players often play for longer than they intended to. In the most recent findings, published in 2007, Mark Griffiths examined the way games can make you lose track of time. Using the results of a 280-person survey, he found that whatever the type of game people liked to play, they often reported 'time loss'. This is characteristic of the sense of immersion and engagement in an experience that psychologists term 'flow'. The games most strongly associated with the time-warping phenomenon were those with complex and compelling goals and levels; plot-driven stories and interaction with other players.

The need to have 'one more go' at solving a puzzle or level was another factor that players often mentioned: the reward cycle showing up again as a motivating reason to keep on playing. 'It becomes almost like a drug, you crave playing it more, and as it's in real time, hours of your life just get sucked away', said Henry, 39, a Lego Star Wars II player.

For some the sense of losing time was a prime reason for playing: one woman even said that she'd been helped to give up smoking because she'd been immersed in a game for hours, and hadn't noticed her cravings. Some players felt guilt at 'wasting time' in a game. 'In my own life I play a lot of games – it's too addictive, I can spend hours', one gamer told me. 'Afterwards I feel a bit "dirty".'

Mark Griffiths also points out that in some circumstances, gaming is a good alternative to other options. 'People pathologise gaming and say it's sad. But if you're unemployed and you can't afford to go out, or go drinking, it can be something very positive and social – and affordable – to do with your time.'

A Global Obsession

Although only a small proportion of gamers develop bona fide addictions, many people seem to be seeking help to combat problem play. 'There's a difference between the people who are checking in for treatment because they are addicted, and those who are there because their partner says they play too much, for example', says Mark Griffiths. 'They're trying to keep their relationship together.'

Addicted All Over the World

Everyone's at risk of problem gaming, it seems. In the UK, Finland, Sweden, USA, South Korea, China . . . addicts or their families are seeking help for an obsession with games.

- In November 2006, a 16-year-old UK teenager was among the first children to be treated for addiction to computer games at Europe's first game addiction clinic in Amsterdam. The Wild Horses Center set up its game addiction programme in response to the number of patients with a compulsion to play games to the detriment of other areas of life. Symptoms of withdrawal from gaming can include 'anxiety, panic attacks, sleep problems, dreaming about games, nightmares, shaking', according to director Keith Bakker. Gaming 'can get totally out of control. These games can be designed to keep the players going. There's no pay-off; it's like climbing a mountain with no top', he told the BBC.
- In South Korea, more than half the population has broadband Internet access, and there are more than 25,000 cybercafes open 24 hours a day. There's been a rash of game-related deaths, and accusations that more than a third of online users are at risk of addiction. Online counselling services have sprung up, and in April 2007, the first government-sponsored initiative, the Centre for Internet Addiction Prevention and Counselling – opened its doors. It spends time helping addicts visualise their dreams and 'wake up to reality'.

Up to 2.1 million players in South Korea are considered at high risk for addiction. And according to official figures, about 750,000 are already so addicted that they no longer lead normal lives. This group of addicts let education, work, relationships, family and friends suffer, and are heading for unemployment. 'For young Koreans, online games are now a greater threat than alcohol and illegal drugs are for adolescents in the west', Seoul psychiatrist Kim Hyun Soo told *Der Spiegel* in February 2006.

- Researchers have estimated that approximately 1 million Thai citizens under the age of 24 are hooked on online games. On average, they spend 31.5 hours per week exploring their favourite worlds. The Thai government has clamped down on cybercafes, so that young people have to apply for an age-verification ID card at the post office before they play games online. Children aren't allowed in the cybercafes during school hours or after 10 p.m., and are limited to 3 hours of online gaming a day. However, some activists fear that Thailand's cybercafe regulations may be part of a movement towards stricter controls on the Internet.

- A report released by the China National Children's Center claimed that 13% of Chinese Internet users under the age of 18 were addicted to Internet gaming. Official statistics show that the number of Internet users in China reached 123 million in mid-2006. About 15% – or 18 million – are under the age of 18. The Chinese authorities have taken action on game addiction, issuing a directive to game operators to limit young people's time online to 3 hours or less. Online gamers will have to register using their identity cards in order to track their game-play time. Those who fail to comply will have their earned credits halved, and removed entirely if they play for 5 hours.

- In the USA, up to 90% of young people play computer games and as many as 15% of them may be addicted, according to data cited in a 2007 American Medical Association report, although other experts think it's closer to 10%. Clinics now offer treatment to an increasing number of problem players across the country.

- A 30-country survey in 2002 showed that among young people in Estonia, Sweden, Norway, Denmark and Finland, around 20% are spending upwards of 3 hours at the keyboard each day. Boys spent their time in online game-worlds, while girls were more likely to be writing emails and using chatrooms. Indeed, heavy computer users were sometimes using their gameplay as an excuse for putting off their military service. While not a reason in itself to defer their period of service, 'Internet addiction' has been cited by would-be recruits to show they weren't ready to face army life.

Treating Addiction

So what can help those obsessed by gaming? Rather worryingly, psychiatrists completely disagree. Some – for example, the Wild Horses Center in Amsterdam – are very clear in their view 'Once an obsessed gamer, always an obsessed gamer.' At this clinic, compulsive gamers must learn to live without the computer to avoid reactivating old habits.

If you're quitting gaming for good, that's OK, just don't do it 'cold turkey', says psychiatrist Jerald Block, who has worked extensively with game addicts. 'I think very few psychiatrists or therapists understand the importance patients may attach to gaming and online worlds', he told me. He believes that restricting access to games, once a player is obsessed, can be extremely counterproductive. Dr Block wrote powerfully following the Columbine massacre that one trigger to the crimes may have been the fact that the killers had their computer access denied for a period (see Chapter 5, "Can Computer Games Make You Violent?" to read more). 'Therapists were trying to be helpful – it's not an unusual recommendation. But I think it was completely wrong. For one thing, it leaves 20 to 40 hours a week to occupy; that's a tremendous amount of time. You can cut someone off, completely, but you need to do that in a special setting – like a camp or rehab facility.'

Jerald Block has treated about 100 game-obsessed clients and taken some traditional and some radical approaches. One 24-year-old man was a heroin addict who had started drug treatment and begun playing an online role-playing game at the same time. He credited part of his successful recovery to the game, which he had played on average 7 hours a day. Despite the fact that both patient and psychiatrist agreed that he was addicted to the game, the doctor did not attempt to change the situation, in the belief that this would cause a drug relapse.

Another patient, a 38-year-old man with a history of schizophrenia, played an online game for about 6 hours a day, and achieved some status within his guild, or team. Although the psychiatrist recognised that this level of gameplay might cause the patient issues (for example, that he neglected his real-life support circle, or became sleep-deprived), he actively encouraged the man to find ways of turning online success into real-world achievement. He suggested the patient sell the virtual gold he was earning in the games to complement his sporadic earnings.

Other counsellors think it's important to work with addicts so that they can cope online without repeating their destructive behaviour. 'The internet is something we live with and need to use. What we are trying to do here is to control and reduce the time that people spend on the internet', says Lhee Hurn-gyu, an online games addiction counsellor in Korea, reported by BBC News Online.

Isn't Compulsiveness a Deliberate Quality of All Games?

While some gamers struggle to shake off bad gaming habits, game designers actively try to promote games you can't put down. Games are supposed to be addictive, according to many in the industry. 'We're talking about *games*. Recreation. Stuff that people do for fun. Even if it were possible to remove the proverbial nicotine, or addictive ingredient, would we want to?' asks Neils Clark of gaming industry website Gamasutra. 'If it takes the fun out of games, then the answer is probably no.'

And even the simplest games should be designed to play again and again, according to game workshop leader Alun Ward: 'I get groups of teenagers to think through what makes a good game – what's most addictive', he told me. 'We can't compete with World of Warcraft, we're thinking simple – like Tetris. In a CD-ROM game there's an atmosphere to get lost in, a fantasy world with swish graphics. In contrast, these little Flash games are for one person to play, and they need to get in quickly and pick it up. The game needs to be "replayable".'

How does that 'replayable' quality translate into action? As editor of prestigious gaming magazine *Edge*, Margaret Robertson played thousands of games and met their creators. 'When you hear game designers talk, it's about reward, it's about making sure you're praised and rewarded and reinforced, whatever the type of game', she told me.

And let's acknowledge the incredible effect that rewards have on the human brain. 'The problem with gaming is that it's an entire and elaborate mechanism constructed to give you positive feedback on what you're doing', says Margaret. 'It's as if you had a really good book that also pats you on the head every time you finish a page. It's an unparalleled moment when the game gives you accolades. It's incredibly shallow, but these days when so many people go through life without validation; grinding away at their job, they don't feel they're getting anywhere – it can be very potent.'

For some gamers, a real relationship seems to develop between gamer and game, or game machine. Psychologist Barrie Gunter notes that games offer the illusion

Game designers see a game you can't put down as a success. Games workshop leader Alun Ward encourages students to make games you have to keep playing.

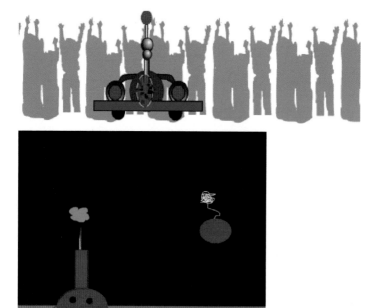

of total control, seeming to pay attention to everything the player says or does. The computer '...may evoke emotional responses from people which are not dissimilar from genuine human interactions.' Sadly, for some people the computer may act in a more friendly and positive way than the people in their real lives.

Psychiatrist Jerald Block has seen that for heavy computer users, their bond with their computer can become as real as their significant relationships in real life. Add this to the deliberately escalating reward-structure of a game and you have a powerful combination.

❙❙ For **heavy computer** users, their **bond** with their **computer** can become **as real as their significant relationships** in real life ❚❚

Are Online Games Particularly All-Consuming?

Online games – the multi-lettered MMOs, or Massively Multiplayer Online games – seem to offer a brighter, shinier hook than many traditional play pursuits. Since the broadband revolution really took hold, millions of players have signed up to take on a customised avatar and spend time in World of Warcraft, EverQuest, RuneScape, Second Life, There and many others.

Online games give people access to communities of like-minded people all over the world – a truly life-enhancing experience for many. 'In real life we go around with barriers around ourselves. In virtual worlds those barriers aren't there', Theresa, a Second Life player, told me. What makes it so engulfing as a game? 'Psychological experience is the backbone of Second Life', she said. 'Over the last few years I've rubbed elbows with artists and businesspeople I would never have met in real life.'

'I think the happy way avatars look and respond makes it a more upbeat place', says Francis_7, a veteran of There. 'Avatars are constantly looking young and cheerful, and I think that tends to present people in a more positive light than how they actually are in real life.' He speculates that this could be the reason so many new players find the experience of There addictive.

For some people this fantasy world becomes something much more than a quick way to let their hair down after work. There are strong psychological elements to playing many multiplayer games – a feeling of escape into a fantasy world in which gamers' experiences are different, and sometimes much better, than reality. Nick Yee, a well-known researcher of online games, says 'On the one hand, there are people for whom the virtual world offers more: social status, a sense of competence and so on. On the other hand, this may lead to the inability to seek out a more fruitful position in the physical world. I think virtual environments can be therapeutic and can offer a safe space for personal growth, but they can also become vicious cycles.'

But a Swedish non-profit organisation, led by parents to help communicate the effects of computer games, also sees positive angles on this aspect of gaming: 'Especially for young boys that don't have a lot of real social life, they go into these online worlds and they get to know lots of people around the world', said Patricia Kempff of Fair Play. 'They get an important identity, and self-esteem, and they are talented so they become somebody for the first time. At 15 this is very important.'

If an online world is friendly and cheerful, is it any surprise people visit again and again?

An owner of a gaming centre in Yucaipa, USA, put it very succinctly: 'In the real world you're just some guy, but in a game, you're the man.'

'We know there are positives and games can be entertaining and educational', explained Patricia Kempff, 'But we wanted to present the risks to parents and also communicate to younger people.'

How can you communicate some of the potential dangers of computer games? In 2006, Swedish non-profit organisation Fair Play, which campaigns to increase public information about gaming, was involved in an annual 48 hour advertising competition. Students aiming for a career in advertising, communication and PR competed to create hard-hitting posters about issues in gaming, which the public and a professional jury then voted on. These are two of the winners.

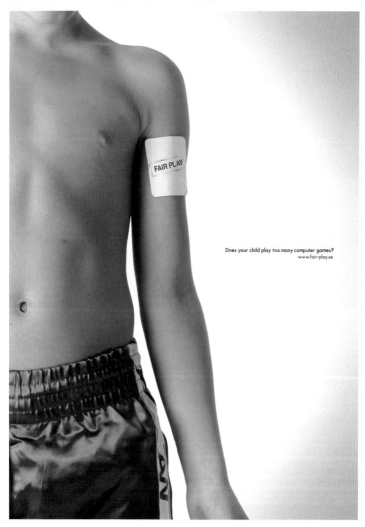

FAIR PLAY

Does your child play too many computer games?
www.fair-play.se

"I'm so happy our son came home drunk last night."

Do you sometimes wish that your child had other interests besides sitting by the computer 24 hours a day?

At Fair-Play you'll not only find information on how to combat computer game abuse, but also tips and advice on how to actually make it a positive part of your child's life.

www.fair-play.se

When Gaming Becomes a Dangerous Obsession

A tiny percentage of the world's millions of online gamers have hit the headline in a series of high-profile stories.

- Texan Joyce Protopapas told CBS News about her 17-year-old son, Michael. In 2 years, computer games transformed him from an outgoing, academically gifted teenager into a reclusive manipulator who dropped out of classes and spent hours day and night playing the multiplayer game World of Warcraft. 'My father was an alcoholic . . . and I saw exactly the same thing in Michael', Protopapas said. 'We battled him until October of last year. We went to therapists, we tried taking the game away. He would threaten us physically. He would curse and call us every name imaginable', she said. 'It was as if he was possessed.' Michael didn't improve until he'd spent 6 months in a therapeutic boarding school.

- Some addiction stories are more horrifying still: one American couple spent so much time playing Dungeons and Dragons online that they neglected their two children almost to the point of starvation. The prosecution said that child neglect because of drug addiction was 'common'. This kind of neglect was rare, but equally serious. The parents 'had food, they just chose not to give it to their kids because they were too busy playing video games' said the prosecuting attorney. The children are now in foster care.

- Lee Seung Seop was a mechanic who repaired boilers by day and played games by night at his local PC Bang – the South Korean equivalent of an Internet cafe. But eventually he lost his girlfriend, then his job, and before long he was spending most of his time gaming online.

In August 2005 he was rushed to hospital after playing real-time strategy game Starcraft non-stop for more than 50 hours. Exhausted and dehydrated, he died of heart failure, his autopsy report recording that 'he forgot to drink.'

■ Few stories are more tragic than that of Shawn Woolley, a 21-year-old with emotional and learning difficulties. He played the multiplayer game EverQuest, finding support and fulfilment online that were missing from his real life. But his mother reported that it eventually led to his breakdown and suicide, after a trusted friend in the game stole all the virtual money and possessions that Shawn had accumulated. A few months later, after a further let-down from his online 'friends', Shawn's mother found him dead, in front of his computer. He had shot himself.

In the months leading up to Shawn's death, his mother had tried all she could to help her son. But she was dismayed by the lack of available resources directly related to online addiction. 'There's no programs for the family sitting on the sideline, racking their brains, trying to figure out how to get their kids off the computer', she told *Wired*. 'I think a treatment program needs to be set up for this that's just as accessible as Alcoholics Anonymous, because I didn't have anywhere to go for help.' She has now set up OnLine Gamers Anonymous to fill the gap.

What Does the Science Say about Online Gaming?

The science of online gaming is a young one – and another area of huge debate. A survey by Mark Griffiths showed that, among 7000 online gamers, 12%

showed at least three signs of addiction – meaning that they would be considered addicts. In the survey Griffiths used six criteria for addiction modified from the World Health Organization's definitions for a dependence syndrome.

The survey questions were completed by a self-selected sample of gamers, most of them male and with an average age of 21. And Mark Griffiths is pretty sure that online games are easier to become obsessed with than off-line: these games have no end, and there's always someone available to play with. There is never a time when the game is over – you can't turn off the computer knowing that you've done all you can. 'Of course the game never switches off; you can't even pause the game', he told computer gaming website GameSpot. 'So if you are really into the gameplay, I can see why a small proportion of people do get hooked and feel like they don't want to leave.'

Some online worlds are addictive even though they break the rules. Social worlds like There have no traditional quests or clans and nothing specific you need to achieve – they shouldn't be successful games at all. Yet many people spend time chatting, creating a pretty avatar, meeting people, choosing outfits and exploring simply, and appropriately, 'because it's there'. The sense of achievement in a 'game' such as this seems to be connected with social success – can you make your mark in a world full of beautiful people?

Something similar applies in other game-worlds. Although raids on the opposing teams might be a significant aspect of life in World of Warcraft, the underlying motivation for some players may be similar to There: 'I would just practise making complicated stuff, and the more I did it, the better my character got at it. I reached the master level of blacksmithing, and once you're there, you become popular', says WoW player Lee-Ping Wang.

Psychiatrist Jerald Block isn't sure that online gaming is any different to off-line. 'I don't think we know if virtual worlds have more psychological effects. One of the errors we make is to talk about Internet addiction. Addictive behaviour in relation to computers has been going on since the 1970s and '80s. Experts recognised it long before people were connected to the Internet.'

The media interest in 'games addiction' may be part of a cultural bias against gaming. Nick Yee points out a mismatch in the way we treat in-world and in-reality events. If someone dies during an online activity, games take the blame. But: 'High school and college students on football teams regularly die during practice, but their deaths are dealt with by the media with a very holistic perspective. The media questions whether the coach set an unreasonably exhausting regimen. The media questions whether the parents saw warning signs . . . They wonder why the school mandates year-round practice that necessitates training in the hot summers . . . And in no time during all this does anyone suggest that football is addictive and caused the deaths.' Football is too normal, too ordinary, too mainstream to cause someone to die through addiction.

Addictive Games, Addictive Personalities?

Computer games use every mechanism they can to keep you playing: an increasing series of rewards, a sense of achievement, a relationship that can become as significant as those with real people, and – in the case of online games – an experience that never ends.

Yet games are clearly not dangerously addictive for most players. It's common to see people going from one addiction to another: gaming, gambling, chain-smoking, binge-drinking. But they don't have a so-called 'addictive personality', according to the experts, they're just trying different strategies to solve an underlying problem. How do we explain who gets addicted to games and who doesn't? It seems to be a matter of timing and vulnerability – and no one is completely immune.

Are Some More Prone than Others?

So why do some people become dangerously obsessed with games, while others have no difficulty switching off? Games do have in-built mechanisms that try to keep us playing, as we have seen. But there doesn't seem to be enough evidence to suggest that games are addictive by nature. It's much more likely that some people become addicted to games. So who succumbs?

'Just like drug use, some people are more prone to addiction than others', says Dr Jerald Block. 'Biology, temperament, and current stressors and supports all probably play a role in determining who is at risk'. Those factors are of crucial importance, believes Jim Orford at the University of Birmingham, UK. He wrote a report on behavioural addictions for the UK Office of Science and Technology in 2006, and told *New Scientist*: 'Almost any of us can become behavioural addicts, given the right exposure, the right timing and so on. But there are multiple causes: our personalities, genetics – it's not simple.'

Reports of pathological gaming in Asia have brought Dr Block to the conclusion that addiction is a very serious issue – particularly among the young. 'China and Korea are reporting millions of kids, all addicted with a disease that interferes during the key developmental years and with one's education', he says. 'It's a problem seen and described in Asia because they don't use home computers or consoles – most people play in Internet cafes, where the behaviour is there for everyone to see'.

So, hidden levels of home-based gaming may be taking their toll in the west, too. Dr Block believes it's a major public health issue: 'It's extremely difficult to treat and has a high relapse rate. I really believe that pathological computer use is a much more important issue than the violent media debate', he says.

❝ I really **believe** that **pathological computer use** is a **much more important** issue than the **violent media debate** ❞

Jerald Block believes another reason the diagnosis of pathological gaming is under-recognised is that it usually exists in the presence of one or more other problems. In one Korean study, addicts had at least one other diagnosis including attention-deficit disorder, depression, conduct disorder or anxiety disorder. 'In the West, when we see these patients we pick up the depression and other co-morbid diagnoses, but we never screen for, and therefore never detect, the pathological computer use. In Asia, they screen for it and find it', he told me.

Some people deliberately select games that they feel have no hold over them. As a mechanism for a quick mental break, one infrequent game-player told me: 'The two games I do play engender no sense of competition in me; I don't check my statistics and exit part-completed games without a second thought. I enjoy the brief distraction; I "reward" myself with a game on the completion of a task or take a break in a longer job', said Susan, 61, a player of card games like Freecell and Spider Solitaire.

Conclusion

We may all be vulnerable to addiction at certain times in life. Games offer very enticing payback for time spent playing them – online worlds particularly so. And games are designed to deliver perfect packages of challenge, achievement and reward, which is what makes them powerful enough to offer intense experiences. It's this very power that means we can easily overdo it. Given other stresses, lack of current 'real-life' social excitement, too much time on our hands, or simply a temporary lack of willpower, we could all be checking ourselves in to addiction clinic central.

In his work mapping the impacts of online gaming on society, Nick Yee finds himself frustrated by the portrayal of 'addiction' in the context of online world. It's a way of avoiding more difficult questions, he says: 'To ask whether teenagers are getting "addicted" to online games is a way of not asking why our schools are failing to engage our children. To ask why some people get "addicted" to their fantasy personas is a way of not asking how we expect people to derive life satis-faction from working at Wal-Mart.'

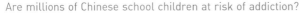

Are millions of Chinese school children at risk of addiction?

PHOTOGRAPHY BY ROB EBERZ, JR

These conclusions apply as much to an online world as to off-line games: some gamers are looking for ways to sweeten the bitter pills they've found life has prescribed. Nick Yee goes on, 'Creating labels such as "online gaming addiction" gives us the illusion that we've identified a new problem in our society instead of talking about the real and chronic problems in the world we live in.'

When it comes to playing computer games, it's odd how quick we are to label it an 'addiction' when other time-consuming activities wriggle off that hook. Is researching your family tree an obsession? You're not trying to avoid issues in the present – you're just fascinated by history. Do you play sport several nights a week and again on Saturdays? Never mind the fact that you never see the kids – you're just keeping fit. Would you rather be seen dead than wearing the wrong shoes, clothes, hairstyle or carrying the wrong bag? Don't worry that you've maxed out 10 store cards – you're interested in fashion.

What's your poison?

5 Can Computer Games Make You Violent?

Introduction

The wildflower known as Rocky Mountain Columbine has delicate blue spring blossoms and a fragrant scent. Discovered in the Colorado mountains in 1820, Columbine was adopted as the official state flower in April 1899. Its common name comes from the Latin *Columba*, meaning dove, a symbol of peace.

Exactly 100 years later, news events at Columbine High School, Littleton, Colorado, brought the word negative associations that it may never shake off. In April 1999, two students killed 13 people and injured 24 more at their school, before committing suicide. The attack, violent and destructive as it was, had been planned on an even larger scale: Eric Harris (18) and Dylan Klebold (17) had planted bombs in the cafeteria, intending to destroy the building and send escaping victims outside into their firing lines. But the bombs failed, and so the two, hiding weapons under black trenchcoats, approached and entered the school building, firing at those they encountered in a 45-minute spree. Shortly after midday, in the school library where they had killed 10 fellow students, they shot themselves.

The Columbine massacre itself has an association that grew up in the immediate aftermath of the tragedy: a link with violent computer games that the two killers were known to play. Other contributing factors gained attention too: bullying at the school and the prevalence of cliques; a copycat effect after watching films like *Natural Born Killers* and *The Basketball Diaries*; the idea that the two boys together fuelled each other's adolescent angst and rage.

But it was Harris' and Klebold's obsession with first-person shooter computer games such as Doom that gained disproportionate and ongoing cultural attention. Guncrime, particularly by young men, has become inextricably linked with media violence – so much so that lawyer Jack Thompson, a vehement US critic of game gore, dramatically predicted that the perpetrator of the Virginia Tech killings in April 2007 would prove to be a game-addict.

The Rocky Mountain Columbine, which blossoms in the spring.

Science and psychology are now shedding light on the question of whether violent games can affect our behaviour. In the relatively new field of computer game research, there is evidence that exposure to violent games may have real physical effects on our brains – at least in the short term. Young people may be more susceptible than others to games' influence. But the fact that only a very few gamers exhibit real-life violent tendencies seems to cast doubt over hasty conclusions of cause and effect – so what can we conclude about Doom and the Columbine killers? This chapter presents what we know – and don't know – about whether games make us aggressive, and whether gamers are likely to act on it.

But it's important to stay within the bounds dictated by the evidence. Jack Thompson's rushed assertion that violent games would be implicated in the case of Seung-Hui Cho, the Virginia Tech shooter, was quashed in a report from the state governor's office in August 2007. The only computer game Cho was known to have played was Sonic the Hedgehog, back in his childhood. Whatever factors had affected Cho's mental state, computer-game violence did not seem to be among them.

Violent Games in the News

It's not hard to find examples of crimes for which computer games have taken the blame. But after the initial finger-pointing, other factors often emerge in relation to the tragedies.

■ In 2002, a 19-year-old student who had been expelled stormed through his school in Erfurt, Germany. Dressed in black with a mask, he shot and killed 16 people and then himself. *Der Spiegel* magazine reported that Robert Steinhauser spent much of his time playing violent computer games, including Counter-Strike in which masked anti-terror units battle to the death. But a classmate said that Steinhauser, who had kept news of his expulsion secret from his family, had clashed with teachers and his parents. The shooting occurred on the day of a school test that would have revealed his deception.

- In 2003, 18-year-old Devin Moore, who had been arrested on suspicion of stealing a car, grabbed a police officer's gun and killed three people before driving away in a patrol car. He reportedly told the police when captured 'Life is like a video game. Everybody's got to die sometime.'

Anti-media-violence crusader Jack Thompson was adamant that Moore's favourite computer game was to blame. He persuaded Moore's lawyers to claim that their client had been programmed to kill, through his repeated playing of Grand Theft Auto (GTA), in which the player steals cars, beats victims to death and shoots police officers.

But the defence was unsuccessful, and in October 2005 Moore was convicted and sentenced to death. Victims' families are pursuing legal action against Sony, Take-Two Interactive, Wal-Mart and GameStop for creating the game and making it available for Moore to buy. Other factors in Moore's actions make it seem likely that his GTA gameplay may have been a retreat from an already awful life. Mental health experts at Moore's trial testified that, at the age of only 20, he suffered from post-traumatic stress disorder (PTSD) after a childhood filled with abuse and neglect. One psychiatrist felt Moore was in a dream-like state, dissociated from reality, when he carried out the shootings. A psychologist, while agreeing with the PTSD diagnosis, nonetheless felt Moore knew what he was doing when he committed his crime.

- In 2004, 14-year-old Stefan Pakeerah lost his life in a hammer attack by a friend who had lured him to secluded woods in Leicester, UK. The 17-year-old boy, named Warren LeBlanc, was accused by Pakeerah's family of being obsessed by the game Manhunt, in which players gain better ratings for performing more gruesome on-screen killings. LeBlanc is serving a life sentence. It transpired later that the game had belonged to the victim Pakeerah, and not the killer.

- Early in 2006, 20-year-old Alexander Koptsev attacked people attending evening prayers at a Moscow synagogue. He injured eight people with a knife, four seriously, before being restrained. Koptsev's father revealed that his son had been playing Postal intensively, a game in which a postman suddenly loses his mind and goes on a stabbing spree in the streets of London. But investigators found anti-Semitic literature among Koptsev's belongings. Now diagnosed with a psychiatric disorder, Koptsev is serving a 16-year sentence.

Can Gamers Tell the Difference between Games and Reality?

Computer games are a lot more realistic than they used to be. Some of my earliest gaming memories are of titles that invited you to believe that a sparsely pixelled cut-out figure was athlete Daley Thompson, or that your character in the adventure game Starquake could teleport between stations that appeared to be rudimentary microwave ovens. By comparison, some of today's games look like footage from the *Ten O'Clock News*. Many games include real-time or pre-rendered imagery that appears incredibly real. So if this imagery shows violent acts – acts in which the player participates – how realistic does the player find it?

In 2005, René Weber began an investigation to try to answer the question. He's in the Department of Communication at the University of California Santa Barbara, and had, for several years, been developing new methods for understanding what media can do to our brains. 'I play first-person shooter games myself', René told me when we spoke. 'I know these games, and I know that when I play, it's just a game.' So with the sceptical view of a gamer, but the neutral perspective of a scientist, he decided to find out whether, on a neurological level, players respond to game violence differently from their response to real.

In his investigation, René and his collaborators used Tactical Ops: Assault on Terror, a realistic-looking game in which players find and kill terrorists, rescue hostages and defuse bombs. In order to peer inside gamers' brains as they played, he wanted to scan them as they played the game within the confines of an fMRI machine. (The technique of functional Magnetic Resonance Imaging seeks to show which areas of the brain are active while engaged in a particular task.) He managed to persuade 13 men aged 18 to 26 to participate – all of them regular 2-hour-a-day gamers.

'We slid people into the scanner, and they played this classic first-person shooter game', René explains. 'Then we did detailed second-by-second content analysis: when they saw blood, when they were shooting, when they were working on a strategy for their next move, and when nothing was happening. We could distinguish scenes when our volunteers acted violently in order to score and win the game, when they acted violently without the purpose of winning, and when they did not act violently.'

> **While** the **players were shooting and killing** in the game they **showed** this characteristic **aggressive** brain activity. **We could identify** a **consistent neurological mechanism** and this was **amazing** for us

What he found was something rather unexpected – news of which spread quickly around the world. 'We actually expected the opposite of what we found', René says. 'When we looked at the fMRI results at moments when there was violent action, we saw similar patterns to those you see in the brains of children with an aggressive behaviour disorder, for example. It was also a similar pattern to what you see when you ask people to think about something that makes them feel really angry and aggressive.' In other words, they'd found evidence that the brain experienced aggression within a first-person shooter game similarly to aggression in real life.

René explained to me what the significance of his finding was: 'It shows a link between playing a first-person shooter game, aggressive cognitions and aggressive affects – brain activity patterns that can represent aggressive thoughts and feelings. We could see that while the players were shooting and killing in the game, they showed this characteristic aggressive brain activity. We could identify a consistent neurological mechanism and this was amazing for us.'

René Weber's research shows that the brain responds to game aggression as it does to real-life strife. The fMRI scans showed characteristic activity in the anterior cingulate cortex and the amygdala – areas associated with decision-making and emotion.

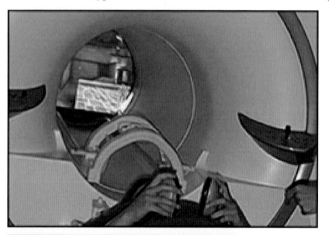

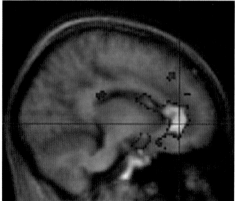

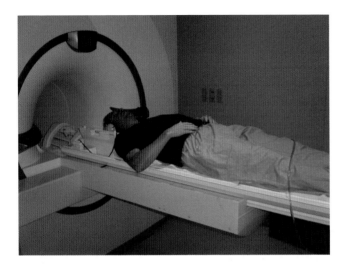

But it's also important to emphasise what the research did *not* demonstrate. 'It does not show that if people play a violent first-person shooter game they act aggressively', he says. 'That would be totally simplified and thus wrong to say. We were looking for a basic neural mechanism.'

Do Aggressive Thoughts Lead to Bad Behaviour?

Brain-wise, a game may make a player exhibit a response to violence. But does that mean they'll go on to act aggressively? This is where it gets complicated.

There are arguments on both sides of the fence, and so far, not enough long-term research that can really say yes or no.

Bruce Bartholow from the University of Missouri-Columbia has investigated the effects of short-term and long-term exposure to violent games. He used a classic technique to measure players' aggression, telling each volunteer that he was taking a reaction-time test against an opponent who he could punish with a blast of loud noise each time he beat him. In fact, volunteers played against a computer which controlled the wins and losses in the game. It isn't always easy to run a study like this: 11 of the 92 participants exhibited signs that they were suspicious they weren't really playing against anyone and had to have their data excluded from the analysis (is anyone studying a link between gaming and the likelihood of being a conspiracy theorist?).

Bartholow also asked participants to play violent first-person shooter Unreal Tournament or non-violent adventure game Myst and then rate their aggression levels, plus their feelings of frustration or achievement in their performance during the experiment. He concluded from his experiments that people who habitually play violent computer games have increased aggression levels – even when you account for the possibility that more naturally aggressive people are attracted to violent games. In the reaction-time test, he found that both those who played Unreal Tournament during the experiment, and habitual players of violent games, delivered louder and longer noise blasts to their fake opponent.

How does Bartholow explain these tendencies to aggression? One answer may be because those who play violent games get desensitised to violent imagery – whether real life or in-game. In a further study, he recruited 39 long-term gamers and gauged their level of violent game-play. He then showed them a stream of pictures including neutral images, negative but non-violent images (e.g. a decomposing animal carcass or ill child) and violent images (e.g. a man pointing a gun at another man's head). By wiring the gamers up to an EEG machine while they viewed the images, the team could see their response in the form of the brain's P300 signal, which measures someone's emotional response to an image – the signal being larger if people are surprised or disturbed by an image, or if something is novel.

In players with the most experience of violent games, Bartholow's team saw a smaller and delayed response to the violent images. 'People who play a lot of violent video games didn't see them as much different from neutral', he told *New Scientist* magazine. Their response was normal for the non-violent, negative scenes but they appeared to be desensitised to violent imagery.

> In **players** with the **most** experience of **violent games,** Bartholow's **team** saw a **smaller** and **delayed response** to the **violent** images

Who's in the Right?

Professor Craig Anderson is a firm believer that game aggression does affect behaviour. He proposes several factors that may make you act aggressively after exposure to media violence. Firstly, he says that if you increase your aggressive thought processes by playing a violent computer game (as René Weber's evidence shows is possible), you're more likely to respond violently if someone mildly provokes you. This is turn reinforces the thought process corresponding to violence. Also, the media violence may make you more physically aroused – your heart rate increases, for example – which tends to allow more violent behaviours to come to the fore. He also believes that the fact of seeing violent acts on the screen encourages you to copy them, and that you will do so if you find yourself in a similar situation.

Many **people disputed** the **interpretation** Anderson **gives** the **research.** Is **the evidence being** "**spun**"?

Based at Iowa State University, Anderson draws his conclusions on the basis of his own published research (see box, 'What Happened Next?') and also on reviews he's made of work published by others, including Bruce Bartholow. His views are widely cited in the USA and abroad, and since they relate to the emotive topics of children, violence and crime, it's pretty important that Anderson's conclusions are robust. Yet, in my research, I found many people who disputed the interpretation Anderson gives the research. Is it possible some evidence is being 'spun'?

René Weber respects Anderson's technique. 'He applies the best social and scientific methodology that's currently available; his and John Sherry's meta-analyses are an important contribution to scientific progress and take into account many scientists' work', he told me. 'I feel Craig Anderson is frequently misinterpreted – perhaps because of his clear and somewhat extreme message. However, while reading his work I sometimes think it would help to understand this new medium of computer games better.'

Psychiatrist Jerald Block is concerned that the evidence shouldn't be presented in a stronger or more long-term light than is justified. 'The aggression studies

Men and women **alike** said Jane might **punch the waiter,** dump the **food** on his **head, steal the cutlery,** swear at the **manager** or think about **setting** the tablecloth **on fire**

are uneven in quality. But most indicate, in my reading, that there is a short-term increase in aggression when you use activating media – TV or games that engage you and have violent content. People get revved up, and can access their anger more easily, but it's short-lived. Long-term there are no clear consequences.'

Mark Griffiths, a psychologist and addiction expert at Nottingham Trent University, explains his sceptical reaction to some of Anderson's claims. 'Craig Anderson states that playing games does make people aggressive but I think the evidence is inconsistent; studies only show a short-term effect, and it's just in the lab. Other things need to be taken into account – for example, aggression in the playground, at home, on TV or in films.'

What Happened Next?

Craig Anderson tested the aggression levels of people who had just played a violent computer game for 20 minutes by using a creative thinking exercise. Participants had to come up with 20 alternative endings to a story in which Jane, who had been working hard all day, went to a restaurant and received extremely slow service. What did violent gameplayers say would happen next as the waiter finally approached? Men and women alike said Jane might punch the waiter, dump the food on his head, steal the cutlery, swear at the manager or think about setting the tablecloth on fire. By comparison, a test group given non-violent games to play suggested similar kinds of thoughts, but fewer violent actions.

Is this evidence that violent gaming leads to violent actions? Experts aren't sure. Would the same results really be seen in real life, not just in the lab? Do the effects last any longer than a few minutes after playing the game?

Psychiatrist Jerald Block feels that Anderson's results can be explained another way: a simple case of allowing someone to get immersed in a game-playing experience and then taking the game away. 'If the game is exciting or entertaining, one might expect them to be angry', he says.

Computer Games and Violence: Unconvincing Evidence

One major problem with computer games research is the comparatively short amount of time games have been around. There's no 50-year data set to which researchers can turn in search of patterns of effect and behaviour. And although research into television has yielded longer-term studies (see the next section, 'What Can We Learn from TV Violence?'), the jury is out as to its parallels with game studies. Should the effects of an interactive game be stronger or weaker than the passive media? You're not just seeing violence on the screen, you're actually committing violent acts, albeit virtual ones. The question is, does this make it any more probable that you'll go on to commit violent acts? Or is this like asking whether playing chess repeatedly will make you try to kill the monarch?

Caroline Pelletier investigates youth and media at the University of London's Institute of Education, and thinks there's a clear distinction between real life and game-play. 'When we kill enemies or cast magic spells in a game, our identification is not with the act of killing or using supernatural powers but with gaining extra points', she told me. 'It is not just that we do not identify with the in-game characters, it is that we cannot – if we did, we could no longer be playful with them, for example, by risking their lives in dangerous situations.'

And gamers I've quizzed agree that the on-screen violence they experience is not what it seems. Even with pretty violent games, when asked what they enjoyed about the game, players cited completely non-violent reasons for liking them: 'Good narrative . . . good graphics . . . excellent atmosphere' (Corrado, 37, Bio-shock – a profoundly story-led but nevertheless violent game); 'Graphics, well balanced gameplay' (Gareth, 32, Resident Evil IV – a shooter that can reportedly involve killing 900 enemies to succeed); 'I like how the graphics of the characters really resembled the Rappers the game is based on' (Rekha, 24, 50 Cent: Bulletproof – in which the protagonist seeks vengeance for a wrong).

Jesper Juul agrees there's a big difference between 'real' violence and game action. Based at the Center for Computer Games Research in Copenhagen, he examines the different aspects of real and fictional play in computer games. He thinks most gamers have no problem appreciating the difference between an on- and off-screen punch. If you use your on-screen character to hit someone else's character, it 'does not mean that one wants to attack that other person in real life: it means that one enters a complex world of symbolic interactions where attacking someone in a game can be an invitation to friendship . . . we cannot take human games at face value.'

That point of view is well stated in this comment on first-person-shooter Marathon: 'I liked it because it was a networked 3D shooter . . . and it let you frag [kill] your friends' (Elias, 38). Could this really be a positive experience? Elias, a gamer now living in Wellington, New Zealand, explained how. 'At a company I worked in, we had a lunchtime Marathon ladder, and the tech support guys used to team up against the design team . . . every day for an hour . . . a fantastic team building exercise.'

Games journalist Margaret Robertson, who revealed her enjoyment of battle-based fantasy game World of Warcraft when I interviewed her, points out the overwhelming physical differences between screen violence and real: 'In a game, you have a constant feedback that this isn't real', she wrote in a recent BBC Online piece. 'In order for someone to get booted in the nuts, you have to press the boot-in-nuts button, and the very act of doing that proves that this isn't real . . . You're wearing slippers and drinking some coffee that's gone a bit cold, not killing a man with your fists.'

A substantial study supports the view that there's no link. The first long-term study of online game violence found no correlation between a highly violent game and real-world aggression. After playing Asheron's Call 2 for an average of 56 hours a month, players were not statistically different from a non-playing control group in their beliefs on aggression, reported researchers from the University of Illinois at Urbana-Champaign, collaborating with the School of Communication and Information at Nanyang Technological University in Singapore. Neither were they more likely to be argumentative with friends or partners after play. To avoid accusations of lab-bias, the study was carried out while people played at home, in the usual gameplay context.

Another large-scale study backs this up. Mark Griffiths, an expert in addictions at Nottingham Trent University, did a study of over 7000 online gamers, looking for evidence of a relationship between excessive time spent playing, and levels of aggression. You might expect that those gamers who play the most would be the most strongly influenced by in-game violence – indeed, the stereotype of the 'loner' game-player with anti-social tendencies persists despite evidence that games now have a wide audience. But here's what the study found: while 11% of the gamers showed signs of addiction (for more details, consult Chapter 4, 'Can Computer Games Turn You into an Addict?'), there was only a weak correlation between aggression and excessive game-play.

What Can We Learn from TV Violence?

Although it seems to have fallen off society's radar, debate raged in the past over whether television violence makes society a nastier place to live. Is there anything to learn about violent computer games from these studies, some of them conducted over several decades?

■ One extremely long-term study confirmed a statistical link between TV viewing and violence in adulthood. In a project lasting a quarter of a century, Columbia University's Jeffrey Johnson tracked the viewing habits of 700 New York State families between 1975 and 2000. He found that those who watched just 1 hour of TV a day were more violent towards other people – a clear link, says Johnson, with the three to five violent acts you're likely to see per hour in primetime schedules. Johnson was careful to account for factors likely to influence the figures: childhood neglect, growing up in a dangerous neighbourhood, low family income and psychiatric problems.

Johnson's research suggested a particularly strong correlation between aggression and TV viewing in young adult women and adolescent males. Indeed, 45% of men who watched three or more hours of TV at age 14 went on to commit an aggressive act. Twenty percent went as far as committing robbery, threatening to injure someone or use a weapon to commit a crime.

■ But despite careful research, it's hard to say how large an effect TV violence has compared to other factors in someone's life. There's strong evidence, for example, that family life affects people's responses to screen violence. A 1986 study published in the journal *Criminology* concluded that the effects of film violence were greater in those who had grown up in violent families.

- It's also possible that violent people are attracted to violent pro- grammes in the first place. A report carried out for the UK's Home Office made a comparison of 82 young offenders (although it did not record whether they had been convicted of violent offences) and 40 non-offenders. Offenders reported higher preferences for violent films, saying that they identified with violent role models. The effects seemed to be long-lasting: evidence during film viewing showed that offenders were more approving of and more interested in violent scenes than non-offenders; 4 and 10 months after viewing the violent film twice as many offenders as non-offenders recalled and identified with vindictively violent characters.

- A school-based study that helped restrict children's time watching television and playing computer games found less exposure made pupils less aggressive. Researchers from Stanford University worked with schools in San José, California, to self-monitor and reduce their use of media. Ultimately, children watched television or played games for less than 1 hour a day in total. Results showed less aggression – in the form of verbal provocation and starting fights – reported and observed among the studied children. However, researchers did not record whether the programmes and games children had previously watched were violent or not. They also had no data on what the chil- dren did instead of watching television each day.

- Another study claimed a link between watching television as a child and the likelihood of becoming a bully. By using existing data from a national US survey, researchers gauged the amount of TV watched by over 1200 4-year-olds. They then looked at subsequent reports of whether the same children went on to become bullies when they were between 6 and 12. Those who watched the most television – 8 hours a day – were three times more likely to become bullies than those who watched none. For children watching the average amount – 3.5 hours – the figure was a quarter more likely than the non-TV-watchers.

Frederick Zimmerman, an economist at the University of Washington in Seattle who led the research, suggested the cause may be desensitisation to violence. The average universally rated movie in the USA might contain over 9 minutes of violent acts – 50% more than in 1940. Just because a programme is made for children, it may not be suitable for 4-year-olds, the research concluded. But is this evidence that television *causes* people to become bullies? It's possible instead that high levels of TV viewing indicate homes where parents are too busy and conflicted to spend much time with their children, where children spend more time occupied in front of a screen than by positive time with adults.

Does television violence lead to real-life aggression?

The Young Minds of Gamers

Is it possible that younger players may interpret the game violence differently to adults? New research says yes. Until 2000, developmental scientists believed that after the first 18 months of life, our brains went into a slow but inevitable decline as unused circuitry was pruned away. But then, a pioneering study carried out by the US National Institute of Mental Health forced a rethink.

The researchers scanned 13 healthy children and teenagers every 2 years as they grew up, for 10 years. By combining the scans, they created movies to visualize

Time-lapse images of combined MRI scans of healthy children from age 5 to 20. Red shows more grey matter: blue less. The prefrontal cortex handles reasoning and is among the latest to mature.

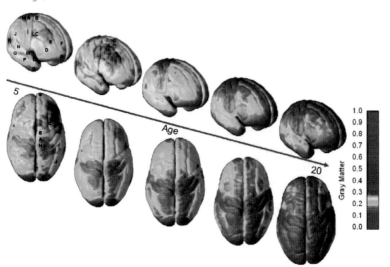

the ebb and flow of the brain's development. Of particular interest was the grey matter – the neurons and their branch-like connections that form the working tissue of the brain's cortex. It had always been thought that the spurt of grey matter growth seen before 18 months was the only one human brains experienced.

The first surprise was that the teenage brains had a second bite at the development cherry. Just before puberty, the children's brains experienced another wave of grey matter production, followed by another round of pruning during the teenage years. This 'use-it-or-lose-it' period, scientists speculated, meant that teenagehood was a crucial time in which to make the most of learning opportunities. It also painted the adolescent mind as a work-in-progress; a period in which the brain underwent huge change along with the body.

The **brain areas** seen to develop last were those **responsible for** reasoning, **integrating sensory information** and **problem-solving**

But then in 2004, another finding emerged. By looking at combined brain scans of children aged 4 to 21, the researchers could see which areas developed earliest, and which remained immature until young adulthood. The first regions to mature were the very front and back of the brain, involved in processing senses and movement. Those involved in spatial orientation and language-learning were next, reaching maturity around the age of 12. But the brain areas seen to develop last were those responsible for reasoning, integrating sensory information and problem-solving. These areas – parts of the prefrontal cortex – weren't really mature until the early twenties.

'We thought that by 8 or 9 years old most of the areas of the cortex were developed', confirms René Weber. 'But now we see that even older adolescents are developing areas of their brain – the decision-making areas and those responsible for emotional functioning. If those areas aren't well-developed, we may not make rational decisions. Adolescents do irrational and riskier things not because they want to, but often because they can't make good decisions.'

> **❝ Adolescents do irrational and riskier things not because they want to** but often because they **can't make** good decisions **❞**

This seems to lend weight to the idea that games could have a particularly strong impact on children. As we've seen, computer games can activate adult brains in patterns of violence. How might this effect be played out in younger people? If the decision-making areas of the human mind aren't fully mature until around 21, could this magnify the effects of violent influences?

Columbine – Why Did It Happen?

Eric Harris was technically an adult, and Dylan Klebold was 5 months away from majority in April 1999 when they committed the series of shootings now known as the Columbine High School massacre. And evidence showed they were hovering between the worlds of child and adult. The lead investigator on the case, Kate Battan, told *Salon* magazine in September 1999: 'The thing that really strikes me about Harris and Klebold, is that sometimes, in the different evidence that we've found, they're so childlike and immature – which is a teenager – and other times they're almost adult-like, which is also a teenager. Sometimes they want to be adult-like and say "It's because we're above all you people", and other times it's "You shouldn't have picked on me". Those are the writings and talkings of kids that are trying to become adults. And they're not being very successful at it.'

> **"** Sometimes, in the different evidence that we've **found, they're so childlike and immature** – which **is** a **teenager** – and **other times** they're almost **adult-like, which is also a teenager "**

In the months following the tragedy, attention inevitably focused on the possible causes leading two run-of-the-mill adolescents to kill 12 students and a teacher, injure 24 other people and then kill themselves. Debate ranged over gun control laws, school bullying and the effects of parental strictness or leniency. Strong feelings over the potential effects of media violence – particularly the first-person shooter Doom – brought computer games into the frame as potential contributory factors to the crimes.

The FBI report released after the attacks at Columbine concluded that none of these potential causes could explain Harris and Klebold's joint actions. The only way to understand what went on was to see the two shooters as separate people with different motivations, said lead investigator and clinical psychologist Dwayne Fusilier. Fusilier labelled Harris, who on the surface was pleasant and well-spoken, as a psychopath, filled with disgust at the inferiority of those around him – clues to which spilled out in his online writings and diary entries. Investigators pointed to Harris's propensity to lie as a clue to his true personality – which, joined with his lack of real remorse at various misdemeanours he committed in his final year, led to the FBI's conclusion that the messianic Harris was the leader of the two. Klebold, in contrast, was depressive and suicidal, prone to outbursts of anger and rage-fuelled fantasies.

Brooks Brown saw the reasons very differently. A close friend of Klebold's, his perspective was as a pupil of the school – and the view wasn't pretty. Bullying was rife: teacher-on-student as well as student-on-student, he says. Elevation of a prized group of 'jocks' above other students by the school administration left some feeling worthless, fuelling rage. Although he confirmed that his schoolmates were computer game fans, Brown saw their appeal to Harris and Klebold as an escape from a world in which nothing made sense. Brooks also blames a lack of police action in response to signs of Eric Harris's increasingly violent activities.

Another View: Virtual Worlds

Yet there is another insight that has emerged into the private lives of Harris and Klebold. It relates to their use of computer games, and yet it is not the standard copycat explanation, or the simplistic reasoning that games imprint a mental script that gamers cannot help but follow. It is not primarily connected either with the effect of violence on a young mind, although this may be a risk factor. The new insight comes from a psychiatrist who has worked extensively with bullied students, with misunderstood patients and – increasingly – with people who've come unstuck with computer games.

Dr Jerald Block started work as an engineer, after a school career that involved regular computer game-playing on an Apple II. It wasn't the only early relationship with technology: his part-time job was selling computers at a local shop. 'I could tell from the clicks as the disk-drive read the floppy whether the boot-up was healthy or flawed', Block told me. At that time, he diagnosed computer problems just by listening. Nowadays, as he hears patients' stories and helps them find out what's troubling them, he has to stay alert to the possibility that they're not always describing events that are taking place in real life.

Dr Block believes few psychiatrists currently understand how important computer gaming and online worlds can be to a patient. 'There are times patients surprise me, too', he says. 'I remember one time when a patient was describing all the relationships she was in, and at the same time complaining about her isolation. I couldn't work it out', he says, 'until I realized they were all virtual relationships'. Patients don't make it obvious when they switch from talking about their 'real' lives to their 'virtual' lives, and so therapists can easily miss the transition. 'To the patient, the two can blend so completely that the distinction between their Virtual and Real existences makes little difference . . . both are "life".'

The virtual world in which the Columbine killers lived was a violent one. Harris and Klebold were committed fans of first-person shooters Doom and Duke Nukem. Harris created new game levels, some of which he distributed for others to play. He showed signs that he found playing the game more real than reality itself, writing (original puncuation retained): 'Doom is so burned into my head my thoughts usually have something to do with the game . . . In fact a dream I had yesterday was about a "Deathmatch" level that I have never even been to. It was so vivid and detailed I will probably try to recreate it using a map editor . . . What I cant do in real life, I try to do in doom . . . The fact is, I love that game and if others tell me "hey, its just a game." I say "ok, I dont care".'

Access Denied

With such a powerful significance, Dr Block's theory is that problems started to build up when the two boys' access to the game was denied. 'Harris and Klebold first started documenting their fantasy of destroying the school when their computer access had been removed', Block told me. 'They'd been arrested for breaking into a vehicle to steal electronics equipment. Harris's father was told by a counsellor that he should restrict his son's computer use for four weeks – not as a punishment, but to try to help him. Eric Harris seemed to be addicted to the computer and his father was told to break the cycle. Almost immediately thereafter, you see both boys erupt in rage and start planning their attack on Columbine.'

‼ Harris and **Klebold** first **started documenting** their **fantasy of destroying** the **school** when their **computer** access had been **removed** 🗗🗗

Families of the two killers were blamed by some for raising out-of-control children. Jerald Block disagrees. 'I don't know what more they could have done. Harris's parents were strict. They cared a lot about their kid and they were engaged with him. They were keeping a log of events and trying to work out how to help him. They did restrict the computer use quite frequently, leading up to this one extended ban.'

'Klebold had very supportive parents; there were other issues going on in the house but they were clearly giving to their child. They were probably the polar opposite of Harris's family in terms of restrictions. When the police went in after the attack, Harris's household had one computer in a room next to his parents' bedroom. It must have been moved to give him less access. But Klebold had several computers in his bedroom.'

Dr Block also discounts bullying as a primary cause for concern – despite Brooks Brown's assertion that it was rife in the school. 'There was bullying in the school. But I've heard a lot about bullying from my patients and, in the cases that we know of at Columbine, I wasn't all that taken by its severity.'

What, then, is the explanation for the boiling rage that Harris certainly experienced, and with which Klebold actively engaged? 'Some aspects of home life may have been a factor – as they are for any adolescent', says Block. 'My sense was they were intelligent kids that immersed themselves into virtual worlds and got no recognition for their [game-world] achievements and accomplishments.' Indeed, their nerdish tendencies made them social outcasts and got them into trouble. 'It started when they hacked into the computer system at the school, and got locker combinations', says Jerald Block, 'A pretty clever sort of prank – but they got caught and were punished by being banned from the computer, which was their life-blood.'

Based on the cases he's seen in his practice, Jerald Block theorises that for heavy computer users, their relationship with their computer becomes as real as their bonds to parents or friends. If that relationship should be severed (in normal life perhaps by a loss of broadband, or time away from the computer during holiday), real feelings of loss and withdrawal can result. When Harris and Klebold became involved in petty crime and – at the advice of expert counsellors – had their computer access restricted by their families, they lost both a significant relationship and an outlet for their rage. In addition, for Harris and Klebold, their sense of achievement and reward was greatest when they were online. Although they were doing well enough at school, they weren't academic stars or football captains. 'There was a discrepancy between the two worlds; in one they were accomplishing things. But there was no recognition of that by the outside world', Block explains. Thus, when their computer access was restricted, nobody would have a real sense of how severe the loss would feel.

When **Harris** and Klebold became **involved in petty crime** and – at the advice of **expert** counselors – had their **computer access restricted by their families,** they **lost** both a **significant relationship** and an **outlet for their rage**

So Harris and Klebold's plans for revenge on an uncaring world took shape. And they viewed the attack as if it would take place in a version of Doom instead of reality. Harris wrote: 'I will force myself to believe that everyone is just another monster from Doom like FH or LS or Demons, so it is either me or them. I have to turn off my feelings. Keep this in mind, I want to burn the world, I want to kill everyone except about 5 people.' FH means *Former Human* and LS *Lost Soul* – monsters within the game. Klebold joined in the revenge fantasy; indeed, he was the first to propose the attack in his diaries.

Harris had previously created Doom levels to resemble the neighbourhood where he and Klebold had carried out some of their antisocial activities. Jerald Block believes that Harris may well have modelled the school in a Doom level as part of the process of planning the attack, although the so-called *Tier* levels of which they might have been a part are now lost. But what's significant according to Dr Block is that by conceiving the planned destruction in his Doom persona, Harris and Klebold were seeking to actualise the merger of their virtual and actual existences. In an attempt to get the real world to appreciate their power in the virtual world, he and Klebold brought deadly force to bear in their real-life school, with devastating effect.

By conceiving the **planned destruction** in his Doom **persona,** Harris and **Klebold** were **seeking to actualise the merger** of their virtual and actual existences

Questions for the Future

The fracture between real and virtual worlds that may have contributed to the Columbine disaster is not the usual explanation for how games may affect our behaviour. But it may be typical of the more complex ideas for which we need to be prepared. There's still a long way to go in discovering the dimensions and nature of the effects of game violence on our minds – and particularly those of our children.

Indeed, what becomes clear is that, in this field of research there is little published evidence that is not hotly disputed by other academics. After carrying out a review of evidence on the impact of violent computer games on young people for the UK's Home Office, researchers at the Stirling Media Research Institute called for a new agenda. The question they posed was not 'Do violent games cause violent behaviour', but: 'Are there combinations of types of games, types of personalities and situations which . . . might cause damage to certain types of (children and young) people in certain circumstances?'

We're shaped much more strongly by the immediate influences on our lives – our schools, our families, our neighbourhoods – than we are by what we see on television or experience in a game, according to the prevailing view of all but the most hardened campaigners. People who live under ongoing stress of any kind are already living with an increased risk of turning to violence whether their minds are exposed to game violence or not.

And we can see that most people are not noticeably affected if they play Doom or Grand Theft Auto. Granted, they may experience a short period after playing when they're still 'pumped up' – reliving some of the cognitions that have caused arousal during gameplay. This effect doesn't even require violence or much activity on the screen. The fact that it's hard to tear yourself away from a comfortable media experience is witnessed every day by parents and teachers whose grumpy charges have been allowed to watch television before school.

And yet, the idea that violent games may affect us at some level is enough to make many people avoid things they sense are unhealthy. It's the same for all media. Personally, I find that what I read affects what I write – and so I avoid reading anything too pulpy if I'm in the middle of a writing project, otherwise my style goes wrong. I similarly find it hard to shake from my mind any creepy TV images I've witnessed after it goes dark.

I'm probably just a sensitive flower. But others feel similarly – especially where children are concerned. 'Where there is a lot of parental supervision, most of the negative effects disappear', says René Weber. He goes on: 'It's a complex phenomenon and there are always questions. But it doesn't prevent us, when it's reasonable, from putting together the pieces.' Other researchers have told me they institute rules with their children – 'particularly the 12-year-old who's just coming across violent computer games', said one. Another doesn't allow into the house games in which real people are targets for violence.

Should we get rid of violent games all together? Although a few campaigners, teachers and parents might disagree, the evidence that banning violent computer games would reduce violent crime seems pretty thin. Plenty of influences come higher up the list of risk factors for violence than an enjoyment of playing computer games.

Indeed, Henry Jenkins, professor of comparative media studies at the Massachusetts Institute of Technology, believes artforms that explore violence and aggression are vital to a healthy society. 'We need art to speak to us about the nature of trauma and loss or of human aggression because these are core aspects of our lives', he says. 'What we want to do is to make sure that our media violence is meaningful and that it encourages some degree of reflection on the place of violence in human societies.'

It would be unthinkable to remove all violent references from books, plays and other media, even those targeted at children: how would school English Literature syllabuses look without Shakespeare or *Lord of the Flies*? 'We [need] open and honest conversations about the place of violence within our culture', says Jenkins, 'Conversations which include the broadest possible range of voices – not simply media reformers and experimental psychologists but also criminologists, cultural critics, anthropologists, and creative artists.'

The Game Police – Ratings and Enforcement

One worrying trend for games is the continuing ignorance that adults display towards the ratings that all off-the-shelf games now carry. Denoting suitability for age, the PEGI system in place across the European Union rates for ages 3+, 7+, 12+, 16+ and 18+. Similar systems operate in the USA and Canada, South Korea, Japan, Australia and New Zealand. The PEGI system is currently voluntary, but under certain conditions (the more graphic end of sex or violence) a game must also be rated by the British Board of Film Classification.

The system is simple enough. But many people choose to ignore its advice. Research presented at the 2005 Entertainment and Leisure Software Publishers

Association (ELSPA) summit in London showed that parents were choosing to let their under-aged children play 18-rated games. 'Parents perceive age ratings as a guide but not as a definite prohibition', explained one speaker. 'Some may have not liked the content but they did not prohibit the game.' Parents were more worried about how long children spent playing, rather than the type of title their children chose.

Further research published in 2005 supported this finding. Among all 8- to 18-year-old gamers (the focus age-group) only one in five said their parents had rules about which games they could play. Consequently, two thirds of all 12- to 16-year-olds said they had played the infamous Grand Theft Auto III – a violent game with an 18 rating. If it turns out that game violence does have a disproportionate effect on young minds, then this is truly something to be concerned about.

One teacher who runs a school breakfast club for 4- to 11-year-olds told me of her experiences with game-ratings: 'The club was burgled last year and the Play-Stations plus all the games were stolen. We had a list of all the games, so a usually responsible person, who was dealing with the insurance side, said they would replace them for us with the same or similar. When the games arrived, we had to return three of them because they were rated for age 15+.'

She has seen the same lax attitude to game suitability among parents, too. 'We have become aware that many parents don't even consider the importance of the age guidance on games – particularly for boys, who are by far and away the main users of the PlayStations. My main concern is the violence – the majority of the games seem to involve zapping – it can be great fun, but some graphics are unbelievable.'

Even for concerned parents, the problem isn't easy to tackle. Free demo versions of many games are available to download online – neatly sidestepping the issue of going into a shop and buying a game that's rated for older users.

Super Columbine Role-Playing-Game

Six years after the notorious events at Columbine High School, a game emerged with the apparently gut-wrenching title Super Columbine Massacre Role Playing Game! (SCMRPG!). The game, which recreated the events of the shootings through the eyes of the two killers, had a low-key launch, gaining media attention when it was banned from the Slamdance Film Festival's 'Guerilla Gamemaker Competition' – even though it had already been selected as a finalist.

Banned for being too violent? In bad taste? On moral grounds? SCMRPG! was, according to its creator, actually a sophisticated piece of work based on a very personal reaction to the Columbine tragedy. The 2-D game used sprite-based characters who move around a top-down plan of the school, shooting and setting off explosions. In stark contrast to its childlike graphics, the gameplay included realistic dialogue taken from the killers' writings and the police reports; voice samples, photographs and video surveillance pictures from the crime scenes including a gruesome photograph of the bodies of Harris and Klebold.

The game's writer, Danny Ledonne, was still at high school when the Columbine shootings took place. He recognised something in the media coverage of the events: the downward spiral of the perpetrators which he felt he might be on the road to repeating. Ledonne had been picked upon since kindergarten and built up a distorted picture of life. 'It was the kind of bullying that most kids who were bullied experienced', he told the Rocky Mountain News. 'When you get pushed every day, and when you are ostracized not once, not twice, but years in and out . . . these things really do warp your understanding and your perception of humanity in some almost irrevocable way.'

Ledonne decided he could do something to help himself: he got into film-making and started seeing a therapist. 'I had thoughts of hurting myself or hurting someone else, and Columbine forced me to take a long hard look at those ideas and walk away from that', he said.

A few years later, Ledonne made SCMRPG! after coming across game-building software. The title lampooned common game titles from the early 1990s, while the very serious stated aim of the game was to challenge players to think about why the massacre happened. Ledonne told the Next Generation website: 'A videogame is a unique way to explore the subject in an interactive way unlike films or books.'

Reaction to the game was understandably strong – some felt it went way beyond what was appropriate, either in its depiction of the events or its continuation of the dark celebrity accorded killers in the media.

But others have called the game 'a deep and complex account' of the events that took place. Ian Bogost, a proponent of games that seek to communicate serious messages, wrote: 'I think the effort is brave, sophisticated, and worthy of praise from those of us interested in video-games with an agenda. The purpose of this game is not to celebrate the events at Columbine, but to attempt to represent them from the per-spective of the perpetrators. This is a worthwhile effort and one truly unique to videogames as a medium.'

▟▟ I think the **effort is brave, sophisticated**, and **worthy of praise** from **those** of **us** interested in **videogames with an agenda**. The **purpose** of this **game** is **not** to **celebrate** the **events at Columbine**, but to **attempt** to represent

them from the **perspective of the perpetrators** ▌▌

One victim of the 1999 shooting, who was left paralysed from the waist down as a result of several wounds, overcame reservations and tried the game. Richard Castaldo reported to MTV that he could see that Ledonne 'was trying [to make] a sort of a documentary in video game form . . . trying to shed some light on what happened.'

Is a computer game any way to cope with the implications of a massacre?

Conclusion

Until there are many more long-term studies, we won't know what factors in someone's life may be linked with an inability to distinguish game reality from real reality. In the field of research into violent games, new models may be needed to try to relate given factors, as the Stirling researchers suggest. Psychological aspects of gaming such as those proposed by Jerald Block give a sophisticated new way of understanding what may be going on.

But maybe there is also a need to explore new game scripts, new ways of playing that take advantage of the power of the medium without resorting to violence as the primary form of action and main realm for achievement. As game critic and designer Ian Bogost remarked in our interview: 'Let's just make games about other things!' He is a proponent of the concept of computer games with an agenda. 'That's an easy solution. Then one cannot dismiss an entire medium on the basis of just a few games.'

Veteran game designer Warren Spector recently criticised ultra-violent games such as Grand Theft Auto for their lack of exploration of non-violent possibilities: 'I am frustrated that the games in the GTA series, some of the finest combinations of pure game design and commercial appeal, offer a fictional package that makes them difficult to hold up as examples of what our medium is capable of achieving', he told an audience at the 2005 Montreal Game Summit.

He went on, 'Sadly . . . most people won't take the time to look past the surface, the fiction, the context. They don't see the fun and the freedom the game provides. They see carjackings and gun battles and hookers. You can talk about game design genius 'til you're blue in the face. The people who want to regulate games, and the mainstream audience we want to reach, will ignore you. And then they'll drop the hammer on our medium. Hard.'

6 Can Computer Games Change the Way You Learn?

Introduction

Tim Rylands found the adventure game Myst by chance. A friend recommended it to him as a way of exercising his 'exploration muscles' while he was recuperating from illness. But the former class teacher at Chew Magna School in Somerset saw how playing the game could inspire children – while boosting their literacy skills.

'It's a shared journey and experience', he explains. 'We're learning together, finding wonderful and unexpected things; picking up ideas and juggling with them.' And by allowing his classes to let their imaginations run freely in the game, he's seen some remarkable gains in their vocabulary, creativity and understanding. 'It's a different way of extending and developing ideas so that even the most reluctant writers feel it's worth recording', Tim tells me. 'One wonderful thing is how boys are writing so much.'

The inspiring game-world of Myst

By **allowing** his classes to let their **imaginations run freely** in the **game,** he's seen **some remarkable gains** in their vocabulary, **creativity** and **understanding**

Tim's also seen improved test scores in English. 'We work out some of the puzzles and then write instructions for other people to follow', he explains. 'We've written poetry, journalistic news-writing, witness reports . . .' He has seen children who normally write just one line come up with remarkable descriptive narrative in the heat of the moment. Now Tim's travelling the world to introduce the idea of learning-through-Myst to a global audience. But what's the game's attraction?

'The Myst games are stunning: totally immersive', Tim says. 'We walk through a game, and describe everything we can see, hear and touch around us.' Sometimes he sits among a class and runs the game as they see it projected on the whiteboard. Other times he passes around the wireless mouse for the children to control.

Tim uses the game to help deliver parts of the literacy curriculum – particularly in creative writing. 'Can anyone give me any similes or metaphors for the colour of that rock?', he says in one lesson. 'Like a white heart', offers one girl. 'It's streaked with scars', says a boy. From time to time, Tim reads from one of the virtual books scattered throughout the game. 'Look, that's a really good use of a comma.' In another lesson he helps the class to explore when to use a new paragraph by comparing it with the actions of turning to look at something new in the game, or picking up an object.

'I am a fan of emergent planning', says Tim, which fits completely with the emergent learning that's going on. 'I don't tell the class what to expect in the lesson. I write down my Learning Objective (LO) on a card and at the end I ask the class what they thought we were doing. And, LO and behold, if I got my lesson right, they'll match.' Games, learning and fun in the classroom – who could ask for more?

A casual glance at computer gaming might leave you believing that it's all a waste of time. Children bashing away on buttons, adults in suspended animation, silent for hours as they stare at a screen.

And yet, there's much more going on than there may appear. Researchers are now suggesting that there are multiple educational benefits to gaming. Whether you're a nursery child, a teacher, a university student or someone taking training courses at work or for fun, games seem to have much to offer. Games have a way of tapping into our natural desires for knowledge and reward – a perfect combination to promote learning.

Computer games genuinely seem to be changing the way we learn. Far from being a passive waste of time, they can help us learn the three Rs. There's real-life learning a-plenty to be had for kids, students, medics and even ex-prisoners – and they can teach in a more natural way than the classroom setting sometimes enables. In this chapter you'll find some of the most imaginative ways in which people are using games to promote new kinds of learning – in the classroom and outside.

We Don't Currently Value Computer Games for Learning

There's a bit of a cultural problem with talking about computer games and learning. For many people, the two concepts just don't fit together. It's a bit like fish and bicycles – they don't need each other; or oil and water – they just don't mix. Some people don't think games merit consideration as learning tools at all, rather as beans on toast don't deserve the finest wines known to humanity.

Computer **games** and learning: for **many people**, it's like **fish and bicycles** – the two **just don't fit** together.

Is it because of an underlying idea that games are flippant things, of no real significance and only for fun? Is it that age-old cultural fear that proper learning can only be done with a scowl on your face and an eye on the test next week?

Screen-based activities do tend to get bad press. We place a higher value on traditional, established pastimes such as reading and playing board games than on any learning outcomes from television or computer games. There's even a fear that, if we let them anywhere near a classroom, computer games may displace these more wholesome, cerebral activities, leading to creeping cultural decline.

The evidence suggests, however, that even those of us who've grown up with a traditional education may not be as committed to the basic skills as we thought. Take reading. Recent research from Manchester University shows that UK adults spend more time reading each day now than we did 30 years ago. Surprised? Impressed? Don't be. We're still only spending 7 minutes a day reading, compared to 4 minutes, three decades ago. If you take newspapers into account you can add one more minute each day – go on, be a devil.

Hmm. Are we doing any better with the maths skills we say we value so highly? *UK adults fail child's maths test* taunted recent headlines, announcing the results of a poll of 2000 adults. While 96% of over-55s got a basic maths problem right (what is one eighth of 32?), 12% of 18- to 25-year-olds got it wrong. The question had been taken from a maths test given to 8-year-olds. Perhaps we're not as committed to mental arithmetic as we had thought, either . . .

For some, this kind of news is evidence that education is, as they say, 'going down the toilet' (see the next section, 'What's the Answer?'). Is it proof that computer games have already started to take their toll? Well, for the adults in these two examples, it seems not. The early part of their school career in which they laid down basic literacy and numeracy skills would have been complete before the first PlayStations arrived in the UK in 1995.

What's the Answer?

What's one eighth of 32? Here's how discussions of the answer unfolded in the online *Scotsman* newspaper.

jennifer   **11:09 a.m. 17 July 2007**

'Is it 4? Speedy mental arithmetic always could put me in a panic. So stopped applying myself.'

Lynn, Madison, Wisconsin, USA   **2:02 p.m. 17 July 2007**

'Jenniifer: Totally correct!!'

jennifer   **2:06 p.m. 17 July 2007**

'Thankyou Linn.'

Turkey Jerky   **3:21 p.m. 17 July 2007**

'You notice that she can't spell Lynn even when staring straight at it as well.
Nor can Lynn spell Jennifer. LOL
Maybe maths isn't their strong point but I suspect languages are also not their strongest either.'

bill1   **11:10 a.m. 18 July 2007**

'No surprise here.

Reading, writing and arithmetic went out of the window a long time ago.

Kids are not taught the essentials any more, school is more about social control than anything else . . . I would not be surprised if a high proportion of the people in the survey could not even understand the question.'

Are our number skills deteriorating?

Games Develop the Three Rs

Could there be the remotest possibility that computer games might actually *help* people to gain their three Rs? It might not seem as though there's an obvious mapping from most games to essential every day skills. But I'd like to suggest that for some games, the link is pretty strong.

In the chapter 'Can Computer Games Change the Way You Think?' we see the evidence that games can enhance your brain's skills in thinking and knowing. Games can help people develop better cognitive abilities like visualisation, mental rotation and rapid multi-tasking.

Now we're looking at the interlinked abilities that we consider make us operational members of society: the fundamental learned skills of literacy and numeracy. Can computer games – the ones you play for fun – have an impact on these, too?

Unlike most television programmes, many games use reading as a key task. It might be a way for the game-makers to reveal clues to you, like the leather-bound volumes you'd find scattered around the worlds of the Myst series. It might be in emails and information hacked from computers in the cyberpunk role-playing game Deus Ex. For children, in the game Animal Crossing, there's not only reading but also writing, as they send and receive notes and gifts. James Paul Gee, author of *What Video Games Have to Teach Us about Learning and Literacy* notes that the same game has helped pre-school children learn English as a second language.

Reading is a skill that unlocks further learning. Without vocabulary and the ability to manipulate meanings and communicate effectively, we'll struggle in the classroom, in the shops, at the job centre – in fact anywhere in our literary culture. So a game that encourages interaction with other players and increased language-learning makes a player more literate.

Darren works for arcade machine supplier Quasimoto in California. In a wonderful blog entry, he lists words he's learned over the course of his life solely through their mention in games. Among them is the word *adjacent*, learned from playing the exclusively text-based Multi-User-Dungeons. From the Exile series of role-playing games he garnered *adept* ('I can't remember what skills I was adept in, but now I use this word all the time', he says). Diablo I and II yield *ethereal*, while the World of Warcraft crop includes the bloody *eviscerate* but also the more conciliatory *mitigate*.

Constance Steinkuehler is a games researcher at the University of Wisconsin-Madison. 'Games are a really interesting place to work because, believe it or not, under the veneer of fantasy, you are looking at a very powerful form of cognition', she tells me. In her masters thesis on learning in Massively Multiplayer Online games (MMOs) she looked at Lineage, an online game that involved players in conducting sieges and defending castles. The content sounds whimsical, but in fact, players engage in research, map-making, resource management, strategy design, debating and discussion. Most of these activities they achieve through writing. Not just a little bit. 'Tons of writing', she says.

> **▌▌ Games** are a **really interesting** place to **work** because, **believe** it or **not**, under the **veneer of fantasy,** you are looking at a **very powerful form** of **cognition ▌▌**

And she's also seen evidence of maths creeping in to MMO games: in this case, World of Warcraft. 'A lot of people hate maths', she says. 'But within the minutiae of World of Warcraft is something called down-ranking. We saw players debating the way it works, and ended up with very complicated conversation about how the maths is worked out, spontaneously debating: "Listen, a percentage of a number, if it is a larger number, is a bigger number." And this is all around elves and crafts in a game.'

Games in the Classroom

So some people are learning things through playing games for fun – without even meaning to. But what happens if a teacher takes games into the classroom with a particular learning aim in mind? Can games work in a formal setting where you've got lots more people and less time than you would have at home?

It is working in some places – for sure. School Tycoon is one of a number of simulation-type games that teachers have tried in their lessons. At Park View City Learning Centre in Birmingham, three groups of 30 10- to 11-year-old pupils played the 'sandbox' version of the game in which you can develop a school from scratch – classrooms, landscaping, recruiting staff and attracting pupils. The 24 challenges of the usual gameplay take too long for a classroom setting, but the 'try it and see' approach seemed to work as a 1-hour alternative. Teachers reported that students learned about spatial thinking, numeracy and social awareness, a finding that was echoed in my survey by Connor, 13, who said that playing the sim-game Rollercoaster Tycoon had taught him 'about money' and to 'be the manager of something'.

In East Riding, Yorkshire, Joy Thompson has been using Zoo Tycoon with classes aged 9–11 at St Nicholas School. Joy has found rewarding results with all abilities of children. She uses the game several times a week for 15-minute sessions in which she passes the radio mouse around so that control is shared. Two baby penguins have been one of the popular outcomes in the school's virtual establishment.

Another simulation game that's been tested in several American schools is the historical empire-building strategy game Civilization III. Kurt Squire, who researches educational communications technology at the University of Wisconsin-Madison, has studied the results in detail. Interestingly, bringing the game into the classroom – both for high school (secondary) and middle school children – did not reap immediate motivational rewards, and many found the game too hard. But for a quarter of the class, who were normally academic underachievers, the game was a huge hit.

Parkside Community College, Cambridge, used Harry Potter and the Chamber of Secrets as a media literacy tool. Teacher James Durran led the 12- to 13-year-olds in a critical comparison of the game with the film portrayal of key moments in the story. Of course, this involved actually playing part of the game, with one student directing and another controlling the game on the interactive whiteboard.

Recently reported from Japan is the way schools are starting to use Nintendo Dual Screen handheld games machines in the classroom – particularly for language learning. By using the stylus to write the English words they hear, and having them corrected by the software, students are performing much better in tests. Nearly 80% reached a good level of English vocabulary where only 18% had succeeded previously. 'These exercises feel like a game', said one student.

At University level, the online world EverQuest provided a virtual culture for real-life ethnography students to study. Instead of a textbook, each student bought a 3-month subscription to the game, and learned how to use data collection techniques in-world. Second Life, an online world that allows user-created construction, was a natural location for a taught course in computer game design. Both experimental projects yielded good student feedback, one participant commenting: 'Through play, I was able to learn on a transparent level. I learned without the pain.'

> **Through play,** I was able to **learn on a transparent level.** I learned without the **pain**

Games in After-School Clubs

Computer games have a place in the relaxed surroundings of after-school clubs – but do they have an educational reason to be there? As I was researching this chapter, I came across an activity programme called MindLab, used in schools and after-school activities. Their materials talked about game-playing and its benefits – a perfect example, as I thought, of using computer games in an educational setting. I called Suri Poulos, Managing Director of MindLab Europe.

But as our conversation developed, it transpired that she wasn't talking about computer games at all. No, the basis of the MindLab system is traditional board games such as chess, draughts, bridge and thinking games from around the world, which, according to Poulos 'families just don't play any more. Children come here to play with other children instead of being glued to the computer or TV.'

I asked Suri about her views on computer games and she graciously admitted that her own children are fans. 'My children do play a lot of computer games – they develop hand-eye coordination, speed, there are some where you have to remember pathways and passwords. But you get that in bridge, for example, as well as needing to master additional skills like communication, reading body language, planning, predicting and working as a team.'

In MindLab, she said, the thinking games create an enjoyable and engaging environment for learning so that children want to learn more and play better. 'MindLab teachers then use the games to teach skills such as thinking, social and emotional intelligence [EI] skills. All the data shows that life's stars are those with strong EI skills.' Board games, in combination with their curriculum, are a great way to develop EI. And what about computer games? Do they use those?

'You just can't learn to manage anger from a computer', said Suri.

For another view, I turned to a primary teacher with many years' experience running before- and after-school activities. Would she see computer games simply as a necessary evil? Not at all. 'The EyeToy is great fun in general and fantastic for coordination, agility, hyperactivity . . . It's one of the games that does get the girls and boys interacting.'

There was learning going on – in the context of good behaviour, socialisation and negotiation. Maybe even some anger management.

'The club has proven that children from Reception to age 11 can discuss and share – it was hard at first but they soon learnt that regular arguments meant no Play-Station! Younger children have learnt to take their turn and share. They have learnt to listen – as have the older boys.'

Games to Teach

What role can computer games play in schools? In my day, 'games in the classroom' would have made sense only on the last day of term when we all piled in with our battered editions of Connect Four, Mousetrap and Operation and spent the day arguing over whose turn it was to throw the dice. Of course, I realise now that our teachers were just trying to get us to develop higher levels of emotional intelligence. But should computer games have a place in primary or secondary schools?

Traditionally, games designed for 'edutainment' were a poor cousin to the games made for the mass-market. But one big factor challenging this is the availability of highly polished and free online games with a broadly educational goal. My son, age 5, recently came back from school having learned to count to 10 in Welsh. Under cross-examination as to how this had been achieved, he revealed a combination of a Welsh-speaking teacher and a jolly online game called Snapdragon, freely available from the BBC, which they had all been playing together on the interactive whiteboard.

A quick survey of the games I've become aware of so far – and remember this is just for the young primary audience – includes excellent quick-hit games from NickJr, The Wiggles, the BBC and Noggin. You can match shapes, make soup, take care of a dog, build a robot, play music, do special effects or a thousand other things. *The Upside Down Show* – which taught 5-year-old Jonathan the words 'horizontal' and 'vertical' – offers a particularly ingenious widget called *Schmancy Schmashup*, in which you draw a picture that is then incorporated, real-time, into an action video with the two funky presenters. Even as the amateur classroom helper that I am, I can see how these games could easily help teach or reinforce important principles.

The Upside Down Show **taught** 5-year-old **Jonathan** the words **horizontal** and **vertical**

Another kind of classroom game that seems to be getting results is online subscription software like Mathletics. At Prince Albert Primary School in Aston,

Birmingham, they're using this maths quiz game to motivate children in numeracy. Mathletics is now used by nearly 1 million students worldwide, who enjoy the benefit of competing with others at their own level from anywhere around the world. Behind the scenes, teachers can track pupils' progress unobtrusively.

The school has found that it becomes a matter of pride to become good at times tables if this means you're going to improve your status as a Mathlete. Gill Gibbs, the maths coordinator at Prince Albert explained to me: 'It's the Mary Poppins approach – turning maths into a game. They're not aware they're learning. In maths, it's not enough to be able to work out what 3×7 is, you need to *know*. The children's speed and accuracy is increasing. It's addictive.'

It's the **Mary Poppins** approach – turning maths **into a game**

The school has found this game has unexpected spin-offs, too. 'One of our lowest-ability boys had hardly any English and low self-esteem', Gill told me. 'He would only say 'yes', 'no', one-word answers. He is now seventh on the Mathletics leader board and he's answered 60,000 questions. He's also initiating conversations.'

Education City is another subscription-based game the school uses. Two 8-year-olds demonstrated it to me: 'It helps me with my homework', says one. 'You have to log-in . . . then you go to activities. My favourite is literacy.' Just what you want to hear.

Technology Everywhere

Mike Farmer is a governor at Prince Albert, where technology pervades every class from the foundation stage upwards. For him, it's all about developing the basic skills that allow learning to happen.

'In our nursery, we give the children easy-to-use video cameras. They run around making videos of each other and then displaying them on the interactive white board', he told me when I visited the school. 'Here we try to give kids a chance to understand what technology can do for them right from the beginning. We've got telephones in the nursery so that kids can telephone each other and learn to communicate better. Most of them are using English as a second language. It develops the skills: then you start learning.'

Mike introduced me to Kalie Sandhu, the nursery specialist at Prince Albert, who explained more: 'We found the children were very interested in the staff phone. So we bought a cordless phone and plugged it in, in two places', Kaie explained. 'In November or December we had some children who just wouldn't talk. The phone rang and I gave it to one child who impulsively said "hello", because someone was speaking at the other end. In real life you don't talk into a phone with no one there. This real phone helped him grow in confidence. One child said "I'll get it" when the phone rang – he'd forgotten he wasn't at home. The barriers came down and he realised it was OK to speak.'

I watched three nursery children, two girls and a boy, playing with the interactive whiteboard. One girl, holding a datapen, leaped up and down to reach all corners of the board, selecting a game while the others pointed and commented. She then began to guide a boat confidently between two banks of reeds on a CBeebies game site.

Kalie went on, 'We want to use ICT [Information and Communication Technology] positively. They're always at a stage of learning, whether it's sensory – touching, feeling, switching on and off for a purpose. If they are comfortable with ICT and technology handling, they will be confident to be able to pick up skills later.'

Further up in the school, children are using Educational Digital Assistants – the school-jargon for personal digital assistants – as a personal learning tool. They

Prince Albert School believes in getting the whole family involved in IT.

can video bits of a lesson to show to parents later, or to post on a class website. Mike Farmer sees this as very different from a PC. 'Computers are a family possession. The EDA is something you put in your pocket like a telephone – it's a powerful personal tool.'

The school uses a piece of game-based software to teach typing: 'We're having a competition to see who can type the fastest after using the program – there is a series of games to use the keyboard faster. Some children type with one finger – it's such a waste of time. We want our kids almost to be touch-typing as they leave primary school. It's a key skill for the future.'

Mike is rolling out an ever-expanding project to lend PCs to local families and connect them to the school's Internet connection via a giant wireless network.

They've seen amazing results, with children teaching their parents how to use the web, getting more involved with homework and even using the computer to run businesses and download Bollywood classics. But the thinking behind the rollout is clear. 'By giving PC access at home, the schools can move this skills development home instead of having to do it at school. Playing games on the computer is part of that and we don't discourage it. It means the school can become a creative centre, freeing teachers to do their jobs creatively.'

> ❝ They've seen **amazing results,** with **children** teaching **their parents** how to **use the web** and getting **more involved** with **homework** ❞

Chemical Leak on Campus!

Kurt Squire has pioneered 'augmented reality' games for schools and universities in his projects at the University of Wisconsin-Madison. For him, learning is best done on the job. I interviewed him about a game called Environmental Detectives in which first-year university students take on the role of a professional investigator charged with tackling a chemical spill on campus. The game is mediated through a hand-held computer that gives players access to the game's stories, plus data, interviews and other resources which they can find through physical exploration.

Do you think students viewed Environmental Detectives as a computer game?

Oh yes – the game contains most of the 'core' features of games: challenges, roles, fantasy, and so on. What I find is really most important is this 'ludic spirit', or spirit of play. The game actually does this pretty well; it takes your everyday surroundings and says, 'What if something really different – like a chemical spill – happened here – and what would we do about it?'. Environmental Detectives (ED) had this urgency that worked well for MIT kids.

One aim of the game is to get students to see the world like an expert, in this case an environmental investigator. But how much do you have to simplify the simulated situation to make it comprehensible? Does this still make it valid?

Well, that's a great point. ED was originally designed for freshmen MIT students who were enrolled in environmental engineering classes. Our more recent games are more geared toward middle school literacy – trying to get kids who aren't reading to read, using the professions as one model. We do make lots of simplifications – and in fact we don't really claim to have any real fidelity to what the scientists actually do on a day to day level; we are more taking examples that are engaging and get them involved in complex thinking. Our real model for 'expertise' is based much more on democratic type principles; we want our kids using language and literacy as ways of representing themselves in the world.

Environmental engineering seems like a particularly good subject for an augmented reality game because of its social dimensions. But in more abstract science learning, are there the right kind of dilemmas and problems to tackle?

Yes and no. We don't think that augmented reality games are a be all and end all to everything. Abstract chemistry, for example, is something that is probably best done another way. Our current work is moving much more toward using the environment as a sort of scaffolding, and making the games truly about that specific place. We want kids to walk away from the games thinking about how they can change the world. So, you'll see that we have a lot of games about land and resource management and urban renewal. Now, it's possible that one could learn more abstracted chemistry in the process of doing one of these games but it would be more a side bar.

You quote one student saying that his socks got wet during the investigation. On the whole, did students enjoy the investigation? Or did they find it uncomfortable, intellectually or physically?

They enjoyed it. We find that just simply getting outside is a huge motivator for kids. It's surprising how much most kids do not like school at all.

One group failed to make sense of the physical and intellectual problem they had to solve. Do we know enough about how to brief a class on what to expect and do in this new learning situation (to avoid a new kind of failure!)?

Well, my research is mostly 'experimental' in the sense that once we know how to brief a class and so on, my work is done and we move on to a new problem – so in a sense, no we don't, otherwise I wouldn't be researching it! It's important to remember here, that 'traditional' school fails most of the time for most kids. In this case, it was 'ok' that the kids failed; failure is a part of learning in gaming.

Do you believe this kind of 'real world' approach to learning should work with all learners because everyone lives in the real world?

Yes – in my mind, this is how people learn best. I think that the kinds of situated learning approaches that we're using are, generally, how people learn best for most things.

Learning Through Games – By Making Your Own

If you don't like the games you see for sale – why not make a better one? User-generated content is now all the rage in many cyber-spheres. Photo-sharing site Flickr, video-streaming site YouTube, the phenomenon that is FaceBook –

none would work without fresh participants sharing their creative ideas, knowledge and feedback every day.

Schools and organisations are now putting the power of game-making into students' hands. Alun Ward is a graphic designer and programmer who works with schools, and also with the Animation Station, a youth-focused multimedia project based in Oxfordshire, UK.

'I run a one-day course that shows how to create a Space-Invaders-type Flash game', Alun told me. 'It's a good introduction to programming and it uses industry-standard tools. The kids create the game designs, do original drawings, and choose the music. They tend to be interested in finding out how games are made, but don't necessarily realise it's a programming course. Of course some just want to play computer games – that's not really what the course is about.'

Alun has also used games in school classes. 'Flash is a good tool for schools: you create something graphical on the screen and then you can keep testing what happens using the code. There's a big community on the internet and you can get example sounds and bits of code.' It chimes with his own earliest experiences of programming: 'I remember the Spectrum games. The first time you made something move on the screen, using code, it was a little bit of magic.'

New Games for Learning: MissionMaker

New tools are constantly emerging to allow game-making in the classroom. The magic of being in control is one of the ideas behind an innovative project that brings game-making into students' hands. 'It's very strange', says Caroline Pelletier, 'that most computers come with a video editing package and a photo editing package. But there's nothing that lets you make your own computer games with the same degree of control and quality.'

She recently completed a 3-year project, Making Games, run in collaboration with Immersive Education, a specialist educational software publisher. For her, knowing how to create a computer game is a matter of literacy. 'Many people *play* games, but it is only relatively recently that people have started to give serious thought to how games work, and why people play them. We were interested in getting young people to study how games work in terms of pleasure, persuasion, or marketing across different platforms.'

❝❝ We were **interested** in getting **young people** to **study how games work** in terms of pleasure, persuasion, or **marketing** ❞❞

Why do you need to make a game to be able to analyse it? Caroline explains 'It's an extension of the argument that writing in English makes you familiar with the textual conventions that exist by turning you into a producer of a text.' And computer games are contemporary texts that kids meet in everyday life, so, the argument goes, we should study them alongside books, advertising and newspapers.

The team, from the London Knowledge Lab, began the project by analysing board games – Cluedo, Snakes and Ladders, chess. 'We wanted to understand better the principles according to which games are designed, and why some designs seem to work better than others', says Caroline. 'What makes chess work as a system of interrelated parts?' And what happens if you increase the amount of money you get in Monopoly when you pass Go? We found it upsets the balance – the game could go on forever.'

Armed with this understanding, they set out to build a software tool for making games that anyone can pick up and use – just as you can with video editing software. 'We worked with Immersive Education to allow the kids to create their own settings, write game rules, and design characters who can talk and fight. We tested prototypes with teachers and classes, working with groups of kids from two different schools over three years. We wanted the children's games to look and play like the big commercial titles they are familiar with.'

And the result was MissionMaker, a tool that supports the creation of action-adventure games in 3-D worlds, and which can include video, music and still imagery. It's being used by over 50 schools. What have children learnt by using the software? 'They learned how interactive spaces work – how you use space, colour and sound and other communication modes to make a text. And how to write engaging dialogue as part of a gripping narrative.' More deeply than that, it's a way of developing understanding of how texts work, particularly dramatic, interactive texts.

'But it's also political', says Caroline. 'It gives children the resources and skills to enable them to become sophisticated participants in digital culture, as well as consuming it.'

Games to Teach: Newtoon

Less glossy, but more speedy and portable, is Newtoon, a game-authoring project developed at Futurelab, the education innovator based in Bristol. Newtoon is experimental in two ways, as researcher Jessica Pykett tells me: firstly, it allows students to make their own games in which physics concepts are embedded, which they can then share, play and edit. But secondly, it makes use of the technology that most people already carry around – mobile phones.

MissionMaker is a tool for creating impressive computer games.

can computer games change the way you learn?

'Research suggests that where children construct their own understandings of activities, by authoring games, for example, they may be better able to apply their learning in other contexts', says Jessica. The Newtoon environment will encourage students to follow a pattern of 'play-create-edit'. 'We're using the playful nature of mobile gaming to prompt a sense of curiosity', Jessica explains. 'We want to draw on students' existing knowledge of mobiles, games and science so that they can work things out for themselves, and learn from their mistakes.'

Learning by mistakes is highly memorable – but not always a way that's sanctioned in the context of the classroom. Jessica hopes Newtoon will help students break free of those constraints. 'Making games, we hope, will give people a reason to want to understand physics better, and they can learn playfully and serendipitously through exploring the Newtoon environment.'

There are other hopes for the project, too: 'We'd like to help students to make the connections between physics knowledge and careers in the games or software industry.' Can't argue with that. And Jessica also sees a link between the testing cycle of Newtoon games, and the hypothesise-test-refine of the scientific method and peer review system (other users will be able to rate each game). 'We also want to help students help each other learn, by sharing and editing their creations.'

The final vision for the project is to encourage an online community of mobile gamers who are also physics learners. 'We hope it will prompt people to continue learning on the bus and at home as well as in the classroom', says Jessica. It sounds like a lot more fun than Snake.

Games to Train

If you're a learner who left the classroom behind long ago, games can offer new chances to pick up skills. Since 2002, Caspian Learning has been seeking to integrate learning techniques with computer game technologies to provide training systems that can be rapidly developed. Graeme Duncan, Chief Operating Officer, says 'We believe that games can provide authentic problem-solving experiences. They can improve people's motivation to learn, and their decision-making skills.'

Futurelab's Newtoon project helped create these mobile phone games based around physics principles.

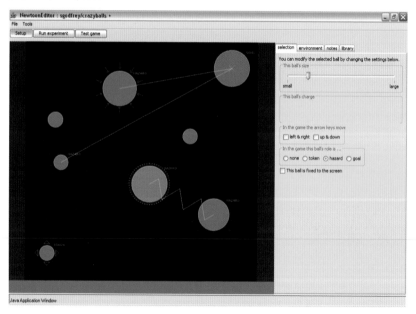

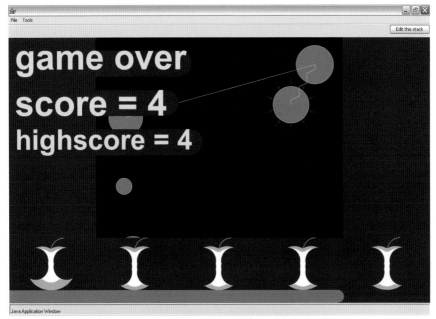

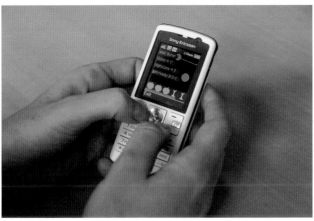

One of the most powerful aspects of simulating a 3-D world, he says, is the way it mitigates risks for the person playing the game. And that's pretty important for one of their current client groups: the hard-to-employ.

For people who have recently left the forces, or prison, or who have recently arrived in the country, getting a job can be extremely challenging. For many, it's intimidating to go to the workplace: what to wear, what to do, who to talk to. 'People end up back at the job centre over and over again because they can't get over the initial anxiety. We've got to try to re-engage them', says Graeme Duncan.

Caspian Learning have developed a Work Experience environment for a client which allows potential employees to explore the workplace without fear of failure. They can explore realistic environments in which work might be available – a vet's surgery, an airport or a construction site among them.

What's the evidence that the training has the desired effect? 'We think about the design in terms of learning from day one', says Graeme. 'It's a learner-controlled environment that increases personalisation. So we see people getting comfortable with the technology. We do a lot to make sure it's suitable – there won't be lots of reading and writing, for example.'

Is it all a bit oversimplified? Graeme insists they don't do any spoonfeeding. 'The player is in charge. They talk to people when they want to: if they feel they're in control they're far more engaged and motivated.'

Caspian Learning is among the many companies, research teams, government departments and education specialists who think computer games are the business when it comes to training. And this is the right trend at the right time, according to John Beck and Mitchell Wade. Their book *Got Game: How the Gamer Generation Is Reshaping Business Forever* has proposed a new view on how the world of work is responding to the 'gamer generation'. If you're currently in your twenties or thirties, and grew up playing games from your earliest memories, it's you they're talking about. Apparently there are 90 million like us in America alone: more than there are baby boomers.

If they feel they're in control they're far more engaged and motivated

Beck and Wade propose that gamers think differently to their managers and bosses in the workplace, with different attitudes to society, risk, values, teamwork and so on. 'All those hours immersed in game culture have created masses of employees with unique attributes: bold but measured risk-taking, an amazing ability to multi-task, and unexpected leadership skills', says the book's blurb. You may see yourself in this description, or you may think it sounds like your horoscope for last Thursday. But if our culture is changing because of the influence of computer games on our development – which I firmly believe it is, even if not in quite the same way as Beck and Wade – then in terms of learning and training, they may be on to something. Triage Trainer is a training game produced by TruSim, a division of Blitz Games Ltd, makers of games as varied as Reservoir Dogs and Bratz and based in Warwickshire, UK. Strategy Director Mary Matthews told me about how they developed the software:

'In our training games, our aim is to produce the level of fidelity that's most appropriate, plus a scenario, characters and setting that will draw people in and engage their attention effectively. The right balance of challenge, risk and reward – just as in an entertainment game – is essential to ensure the game and the learning is completed and continually refreshed through repeated play.'

'All TruSim's staff have worked on leading edge entertainment games. For Triage Trainer we also consulted civilian and military medical experts to ensure that the injuries are accurately represented and that the casualties react emotionally and physically to their injuries as they would in real life. At this level of realism it would be distracting if the characters looked real but did not behave realistically.

'The underlying technology to do this is all based on Blitz Games' own proprietary engine. We developed a simple physiological coded model that drives the characters' breathing, blood circulation and sweating and also movement for the face, eyes, head and body. We have demonstrated the real-time animation of a char-

Blitz Games' Triage Trainer balances the risk and reward of gameplay with extremely realistic injury simulation for effective training.

acter dying from blood loss to doctors who have been so convinced and engaged that they were calling out for someone to help save his life.

'The point of an entertainment game is that is not real life; the point of a serious game is that it can mirror real life and allow the player to make mistakes without harming anyone. The player's mindset in approaching each type will be different but the satisfaction of achieving goals is common to both and it is the skill of the game designer to ensure a player feels the same thrill of success in achieving a learning objective as he or she would in getting to the next level or completing an entertainment game.'

Why Do We Like Learning from Games?

When we do things in life that are fun, improving or otherwise good for us, our brain rewards us to tell us we've done the right thing. It makes perfect evolutionary sense – reinforce our 'good choices' so that we'll survive long enough to do the ultimately pleasurable thing a few times and ensure the species' continuation.

For a long time, scientists thought that the mechanism for this reward belonged with dopamine – 'the brain's pleasure chemical'. But they're rethinking that idea in the light of some evidence that didn't fit the mould.

One researcher noticed that people with a chemical dependency did not seem to experience any real ongoing *pleasure* from their addiction. If the substance of choice released dopamine, wasn't that supposed to be innately rewarding?

And another scientist reran some dopamine-related experiments that had been done on rats. These creatures had had their dopamine circuitry wiped out by a neurotoxin – so they shouldn't have been able to experience the normal reward of eating something nice-tasting. True – the rats showed no interest in looking for any food, and would actually have starved to death if left to their own thoughts. But the strange thing was that when the researcher *forced* the rats to taste something sweet, they responded with pleasure. (If you're in the know, apparently you can read this on their faces.) The animals still *liked* the sweet taste, and felt a reward. But they didn't *want* it – because their dopamine was missing. They weren't going to go out of their way to find it.

And this was what changed the experts' minds about what dopamine really does. In itself it may not be giving the pleasure (opioids may be responsible instead). But dopamine is crucial in motivating us to look for the pleasure in the first place. Neuroscientist Nora Volkow, Director of the US National Institute on Drug Abuse, explains it in these terms: dopamine doesn't only make us feel good. It tells us what's important, what we need to pay attention to. Whether it's danger, food or information, dopamine gives us the urge to engage with the world.

Dopamine doesn't only make us **feel good. It tells us what's important,** what we need to **pay attention** to

There's a connection between our brains' propensity for seeking rewards, and the environment created by computer games. In his bestselling book *Everything Bad is Good for You*, Steven Johnson proposes that games offer a series of rewards that our brains find it hard to resist. 'It's the reward system that draws those players in, and keeps their famously short attention spans locked on the screen. No other form of entertainment offers that cocktail of reward and exploration.'

Simon Egenfeldt-Nielsen, who researches games at the IT University of Copenhagen, describes the brain's drive for gaining knowledge as being like lust. Games, he says, are about exploring and finding out what's behind the next door: basically, we're powerless to resist. If you reap the reward of success – great! If you don't quite make it – the thirst for knowledge kicks in and you sign up for another try.

> ❝ **You can** teach anything, **ANYTHING,** if you make it **into a game** ❞

Eric Newton, who developed complex, content-rich computer games for visitors to the Newseum in Arlington once told me: 'You can teach anything, ANYTHING, if you make it into a game.' He had hit upon a winning formula of content and quest in his games, which taught would-be journalists about the workings of the trade.

What Are We Learning?

Do we learn useful things from games? In some cases, according to one academic, the answer's a straightforward 'no'. Caroline Pelletier, from the London Knowledge Lab, is scathing about some 'edugames'. 'I'm not convinced by some attempts to make curriculum content more exciting by sticking it in a game. You can't treat kids like idiots', she said. 'If the curriculum isn't interesting and exciting there are bigger issues at stake: it's more than putting content in a space invaders jacket.'

So, when the content isn't worth knowing, it's unlikely even the whizziest game in the world could help. On the other hand, sometimes games do actually teach us facts, even if we aren't actively seeking them. My game survey revealed quite a few people who had come away from an entertaining game with knowledge under their belts.

Michael, now 28, reported that he gained 'a better idea at the young age of 12 where different cultures are placed and which world wonders there were' from playing the empire-building Sim Civilization. Rens, 28, said of Civilization IV: 'There are a lot of references to real live people, units, buildings, etc. that's information that sticks and it is fun to look stuff up in Wikipedia about them.'

Alice, 34, told me about the city management game SimCity: 'In some ways it helps me see systems at work. I can see how tweaking one variable affects a whole chain of events.'

Constance Steinkuehler noticed the same thing about some of the gamers she studied. Every time she interviewed a student who played Age of Empires, Civilization or Rome: Total War she would ask them whether they had checked a book out of the college library based on an interest gained by playing the game. About half said they had.

But what if games – at least the games we're playing at the moment – aren't really set up for teaching facts? Might there be other ideas we're picking up?

Constance thinks there's evidence that players of the online role-playing game World of Warcraft are picking up key ideas about the scientific method. 'We did a study of basic science literacy and problem-solving – skills like understanding a system, building models and testing those models', she told me. 'For example, someone might say "I really don't understand how this bit of the mechanics works in the game". Someone else would come up with a theory, then build a model, and compare with other ideas.'

And she was impressed by the overall level of debate that was going on in this massively multiplayer game that attracts a huge age-range in its player profile. 'I visited the game community forums, predicting that 5–10% of the conversations would look like high-end problem solving, and the rest would be banter. The truth was very different. Instead, 86% of a random sample of conversations were about problem-solving.'

Games Can Teach You Life Skills

Practically speaking, can you learn skills from games to take into the real world? Here's one example I just have to mention – particularly as my keyboard skills, although fast, are not typically 100% accurate. The Typing of the Dead is a game in which players defeat zombie hordes by, you're way ahead of me, typing in words and phrases that appear in front of each character. Words begin short, simple and easy to type, and gradually progress to multiple phrases. ('I'm thinking of quitting my job. I've got terrible chest pains. My hearing is nearly gone, too. Testing bullet-proof vests isn't fun.') It sounds very motivating.

Then there are the management skills you can pick up. In games like World of Warcraft there is work experience to be had for those prepared to lead the raiding parties known as guilds. 'It's about learning how to manage friendships', says gamer Margaret Robertson. 'If I saw "running a guild" on someone's CV I'd see it as a demonstration of being a team leader; it's a big and difficult job. I would take it seriously. Just as we are impressed by people who run a hill-walking society, or a jazz band, it's a complex people-management role.'

Learning to work with others is a fact of life for all who've played a co-operative online game – or who have one Wii controller to share between two. 'Games can transform learning experiences. I see it in my own house: grandma interacting with the grandchildren because of computer games', Graeme Duncan tells me. 'My mum's 61 years old, and she and my six-year-old do Brain Training together. The more active and engaged they are, the better the results. They're using the technology, and building skills too – all with smiles on their faces.'

Hard work is a principle in a game like RuneScape, and that's caught the eye of youth researcher Nic Crowe from Brunel University: 'The game is very popular with 11- to 14-year-olds. It's all about character and skills development and we found there was a whole economic substructure running underneath it. Some groups were learning market skills – spotting gaps to exploit, learning about ideas of supply and demand. A couple of people were selling virtual goods for real money', says Nic. But the thing that really went against the usual grain was the amount of *work* these young people were doing. 'Many employers say "These kids can't get into the routine; they can't get up in the morning",' says Nic. 'But we saw children logging on and then going to work for 2 hours – coal mining or fishing, or making armour, or marauding to gather goods. Whatever they considered their work, they did first.'

Are Some Games Too Hard?

Do some games just work us too hard, and present too much of a challenge?
I am no good, for example, at driving games. I try to go too fast; I crash into the
side; I spin so that I am facing backwards; I try to turn around – sometimes using
forward and reverse gears – the other cars all go past me and I quit, discouraged.
I don't think my brain quite 'sees' the motivating rewards perceived by others. I've
certainly rarely had more than one try at a circuit.

So what happens when you try to use a game for teaching – and the students have
to learn the game first? After his pioneering teaching project using the online
world EverQuest, Aaron Delwiche from Trinity University, Texas, wrote about one
downside to his idea. There was an incredibly steep learning curve for those who
hadn't played EverQuest before. One student reported: 'I played EverQuest in class
for about 10 minutes today, and I got killed by a giant bat, a giant spider, a Halfling
named Beardo or something, and I drowned. Sometimes, I stay up at night won-
dering how I got so far in real life.' (Eric, ethnography student)

Alun Ward found Second Life something of a puzzle: 'I tried Second Life – you can
make things and sell them. I spent three hours going around naked, and spoke
to an Italian guy who knew no English. It's not as intuitive as other games, where
there's a defined path. There are many more possibilities.'

❰❰ I spent **three hours** going around naked,
and spoke to an **Italian** guy **who knew no
English** ❰❰

Finding Out the Rules of Games
Is Learning

Because they are a challenge, many games may actually be making us into
better learners. For starters, some scientists think games are all about learning
– when you're gaming, you're learning. A game is based around a set of rules,
decided on by the game designer. But even with relatively simple rules, the designer
can set challenges that are extremely tricky to overcome. The player's role is to
solve the puzzles, or beat the game, by gaining and improving their skills.

Similarly, when you're playing the classic arcade game PacMan you're not just
gobbling dots, says Steven Johnson, you're discerning patterns in the behaviour
of your enemies, and strategising to avoid them. These underlying patterns and
rules are what make games the challenge they are – but also the experience they
can be.

In the driving game Gran Turismo, players certainly have to spend time learning
how to drive the on-screen cars. When you first try this kind of game, whether or
not you're a skilled real-life driver, you'll be fishtailing, spinning and generally
crashing out. What you learn to do by playing is to master the simulation model
the designers have implemented in the game.

Probing a game to discover its rules is something that motivates gamers to play.
In fact, for seasoned players, if the mechanism is too clear, the game's not worth
playing. 'When you ask people why they stopped playing a favourite game, they
often say it was because it had nothing more to teach them (see the next section,
'The Day the Nations Died'). The moment they've figured the system out completely, they're done, and they want a new environment', says Constance Steinkuehler. 'By contrast, if you've ever stood in front of a classroom of kids, they don't
have such a high expectation of learning.'

The Day the Nations Died

Greg loves the real-time strategy game Rise of Nations – as you can see by his time commitment to the game. The game features 18 civilizations which you lead through eight *ages* of world history. But what happens when it all gets a bit too easy?

11:43:42 a.m.
I've started at the edge of the map and pause quickly to get my new house in order – have a check around and set a few things building.

11:49:09 a.m.
Built two new cities, and we're away.

Not seen anything of the opposition as yet – they do tend to scupper my plans by sending small annoying armies to poke at my cities and gradually wear them down.

11:55:55 a.m.
Classical age research complete (1 of 8).

This means I can build exciting new things like universities and mines (yes!).

Still no sign of anyone, but the computer scoring is keeping up with me. Time to put on a spurt.

12:04:48 p.m.
Emperor Manco Capac is on the scene in his nice green uniform.

At this stage of the game it's all about building up as big a nation as you can before anyone comes and blams you out of existence.

I don't build up an army at the beginning because it costs too much resource and stops you from building farms and markets.

12:29:33 p.m.

Things seem to be going slowly. My predicted spurt has not yet hap-pened. I remain cautiously optimistic.

12:41:50 p.m.

Still no-one's come to kill me, but I've found out where the green people come from. They didn't seem overly friendly but haven't sent out search parties to kill my scout.

I am currently in the Gunpowder age (4 of 8).

Started building the Terra Cotta Army, not for its beauty but because it produces troops without costing money.

Nothing in this game is done because it's nice or worthy, only if it benefits you somehow.

12:57:12 p.m.

Under attack!

Those untrustworthy blues have invaded my land and started setting about Lubusi. How disappointing. Fortunately I have a couple of troops sitting about. Better build a barracks quick.

1:01:33 p.m.

The attack has been defeated! Woo!

My army will have time to build up before the next wave comes. Their mistake is to come and attack me, where I can replenish troops quicker than them.

We've struck oil!

1:20:51 p.m.

More battles have ensued – the greens wanted a piece of my ever expanding empire, but fortunately due to my superior technology I was able to beat their horses off with some riflemen.

All is now calm(ish).

I am now at the modern age (7 of 8) and will shortly start on research for the information age.

1:32:54 p.m.

The building commences in earnest – creating oil wells and refineries at will

Resources come pouring in, and enemies are held back for now.

This is the point at which you start to become invincible. Get far enough ahead here and no-one can suppress your information age armies as they roll across their land.

1:46:29 p.m.

Well, I'm thinking about building up a significant army ready to attack those blues that have caused me so much trouble recently. First thing to do is grab the city where they've build the colossus – that gets you +50 population limit.

1:52:29 p.m.

Me: Age 8
Green: Age 6–7
Blue: Age 6–7
Red: Age 6

1:57:28 p.m.

Space programme wonder shows me where every unit is on the map giving me tactical advantage (and somewhere to aim my soon-to-be created nuclear weapons!)

2:00:35 p.m.

Stealth attack by the reds!

Luckily I had a selection of tanks sitting in that area in case such an attack came. Again, technology should win this battle (my 6 tanks to their 25) but I'll create a few more just in case.

[pause for church]

6:15:38 p.m.

The war with enemy Chac Balam begins.

City on the outskirts easily taken with artillery followed up by assault infantry. Now we can expect some retaliation!

6:22:20 p.m.

Colossus captured! I can now build 50 more units!

6:26:27 p.m.

My attack on the blue people fails and they take back the city containing the Colossus.

Some gentle music tries to make me feel like everything's fine in the world.

Time to rebuild the army and use nuclear weapons to ensure victory.

6:36:08 p.m.

Ok we got that city back and now the blue man has been defeated because I sacked his major city.

6:36:28 p.m.

I must admit to getting a bit bored now, so I've started nuking the green guy (who's also still attacking me) left right and centre, as he's proving to be a bit tricky to shift.

6:44:15 p.m.

My terrible organisation of troops doesn't seem to matter now, as nuclear weapons wreak rather easy havoc on oppositions. I'm in the process of taking the green capital city which will lead to their eventual demise.

6:48:47 p.m.

It's all over for emperor Manco Capac as I research World Government and thereby take over his whole country by having control of the capital.

Suddenly only one adversary remains and it all seems a bit easy.

6:54:55 p.m.

Victory comes suddenly without much of a sense of achievement.

The bland music heralds my win, matching the bland method of nuking everyone into submission without any serious consequences.

Ok, so I've run it a bit close with the 'Armageddon clock' ticking dangerously close to zero, but there's no sign in the victory that it's been sullied by fallout for the next 100 years or my troops coming home with radiation poisoning.

Ah well, that's it for another day. Victory. Again. Is it getting too easy?

Conclusion

It's tragic to think that so many of today's learners might not be getting the right mental challenges at school. For some, maybe the power of today's learning technologies can help, as Mike Farmer believes. For others, like those who enjoyed getting wet socks in Kurt Squire's augmented learning game, we need ways of helping them break out of conventional settings that have lost the ability to inspire.

In years to come, learning might look quite different. 'Online games have reorganized our expectations of what education might be in the future', Constance Steinkuehler told me. 'Parents are starting to realize that it's pointless testing kids on facts. It's an antiquated way to look at it. As long as I know what you're an expert in, I can contact you and ask you what you think.'

What, then, are the key skills? The activity of learning to discern what's going on behind the scenes – the basis for learning in many computer games – is a good facsimile for the higher-level analysis of cultural criticism, science or philosophy. And problem-solving is important: 'it's a twenty-first century skill', says Steinkuehler. 'In a game, there's collective intelligence instead of an authority. This means that you end up with cognition and memory and problem-solving distributed over a group of people networked together.'

There are aspects of that idea I find exciting, and some scary. In some ways it sounds like a community of experts, rather than a group setting out to learn vital basics like reading and writing. However wired our modern world, those skills are still the currency of communication.

And even if contemporary games can teach us useful information and skills, I don't know if I am interested in some of the things you can learn, or the ways games currently reward in-game 'success': I'll never be motivated to learn how to beat a driving game.

But as we've seen throughout this chapter, games have power to teach in ways we find almost irresistible. Like the brain's propensity to absorb information if it's presented in the form of a story, or to respond enthusiastically to something described as 'news', our thirst for mental novelty seems to be unquenchable. I love the idea that a game might challenge me to learn physically, emotionally and mentally, rather than falling back on the age-old concept of textbook-style teaching. And imagine what could happen if in the future, learning is based on compulsively fun play activities, personalised to a student's learning rate, and designed around the brain's natural mechanisms of information-seeking and problem-solving. Sounds suspiciously as though computer games have rather a lot of potential.

Games have power to teach in **ways** we find **almost irresistible**

7 Can Computer Games Change Your Beliefs?

You play games for fun – right? It's something to do when you want to relax, escape the real world, spend some time doing something inconsequential. If so, the screenshot of a game called Darfur is Dying is probably quite shocking. A *game* in which you play a child cheating death in the desert of Sudan? Could this be entertainment? Who would make a game in such poor taste?

Darfur is Dying is one of a new breed of games that seeks to change your mind. Games that campaign, games that persuade, games that try to sell you things or affect what you do. It's a genre that is still finding its feet, and often generates controversy.

But there's a growing body of people who believe that games can and must reach beyond the realm of mere entertainment. Indeed, they propose that games may be the most powerful medium yet conceived for challenging commonly held views; generating informed debate, yes, even *changing the world*. In the world of sophisticated print and TV advertising, editorial cartooning, alternative comedy and sparkling non-fiction bestsellers, you might expect there'd be better ways of communicating a message. But there's something that gives games an edge over most of these other communication modes. It's their ability to take simple relationships and combine them in a system – and then put you, the player, in charge of what happens next. It's a field in which museums turn out to have stolen a march on other media with ground-breaking message-based games that they refer to as 'interactives'.

Darfur is Dying is a game with a serious message.

Games may be the **most powerful** medium yet **conceived** for challenging **commonly held views;** generating informed **debate,** **yes,** even **changing the world**

What can computer games persuade us to do? How effective are games in raising awareness of political and social causes? Would you buy something if a computer game told you to? Companies who are spending thousands on so-called adver-games think you will. Do they make for powerful propaganda – and if so, what if they get into 'the wrong hands'? How are museums involved in the search for the perfect 'game with a meaning'? And if games are supposed to be for fun, how effective are they for putting across serious messages?

Games with Meaning

Ian Bogost is an assistant professor in the School of Literature, Communication and Culture at the Georgia Institute of Technology, USA. He has literally written the book on 'games with a meaning' in his volume *Persuasive Games*. When I spoke to Ian, I asked him whether games don't all carry some kind of meaning. 'It's not always an intentional message, but in all games, the ideology of the creator is represented,' he confirmed. What's new is the number of games that consciously try to communicate something serious to their audience.

Ian chooses to use the term 'persuasive games' for those games – large and small – that carry an intentional message. And it's his belief that they are an incredible tool for achieving that elusive goal that advertisers, evangelists, campaigners and politicians all seek: changing people's minds. 'Videogames appeal to many ages, demographics, social and ethnic backgrounds', he says, 'and they are unique among mass media in that they rely on rule-based interactions for their framework.' Games embody a system, and by interacting with that system we can discover how the system works. By fiddling with the system (in other words, by playing the game), we can see how the different elements of the system relate to each other. It's much more than a passive media experience.

Indeed, Ian has a phrase for what persuasive games do: they have a *procedural rhetoric*. Like other forms of rhetoric, like a speech or an advertisement, these games try to persuade. But they don't use just audio, or just visuals. Games encode a model that works by a set of rules, enabling a persuasive game to embody an idea or an argument that you explore by doing.

The kind of points that games are making is now very broad indeed. Campaigning games aimed at getting your vote. Environmental games designed to make you save energy. Advertising games created to sell products. Memorial games to commemorate victims of a tragedy. Editorial games designed to expose social trends or even scandals.

What makes a good persuasive game? As we'll see, there are several schools of thought on that point. But the field is certainly maturing. 'What we often see in other media is as they evolve they become more sophisticated', says Ian Bogost. 'One piece of media may meet several objectives; for example a film or novel may be entertainment but it may carry a political message too. Now, that process has started to happen in games.'

Games for a Social Cause

Ayiti: The Cost of Life is an awareness-raising online game produced by Playing 4 Keeps, a high-school-based games education project in Brooklyn, USA, in collaboration with New York-based development company Gamelab. Launched in 2006, the game challenges players to keep a family of five in rural Haiti (Ayiti in local language) alive through a 4-year period as they negotiate the often-conflicting goals of earning money, staying healthy and happy, coping with hurricanes and other natural disasters, and going to school. The team of young people involved in developing the game – all of Caribbean descent – chose to focus on Haiti because of the country's multiple problems. 'When you're very poor, you have very few choices', 18-year-old Jonathan Laurent told *The Toronto Star*. 'Sending kids to school means less income. But if you send them to work, it means they lack education and it's hard to get jobs.'

And these difficult decisions are played out in the game. When I first played, four members of the family were dead of cholera by year two. I passed on the link to my husband to try. 'All ill already', he reported over instant messenger (he's a programmer who, as I do, works from home). 'OK everyone died.' He tried a new strategy, choosing 'education' from the four options presented at the start of the game. 'Everyone still got ill. It was going well until the hurricane struck. Maybe I will pay for boarding up the windows this time.' We agreed to this strategy. 'That's worked!' he reported in his next round of play. 'Good thing you had enough money', I typed. 'Yeah – everyone has to work, even the little kid', he told me. 'I'm in the second year, everyone is still alive. But no education.' The window went quiet again. 'OK everyone dead again from TB this time', he reported.

Is the game too hard? Or does it have the tragic message that there's no way out for a family in Haiti's countryside? Other players have reported feeling hopeless after playing Ayiti: 'OK, maybe I am a bad loser, but I really don't think the game gives a very accurate portrait of the living conditions', complained one poster to the Unicef Voice of Youth page. 'Even though I never let the family work hard, they just kept getting sicker and sicker.' Unable to make the game 'deliver', the player started to suspect the game was designed to elicit empathy and cash from players – something they found objectionable. 'It annoys me if a game or media is abused like that, for cheap propaganda (and targeting children, too).'

Ayiti: The Cost of Life – Is it too hard to play this game – and is that the message?

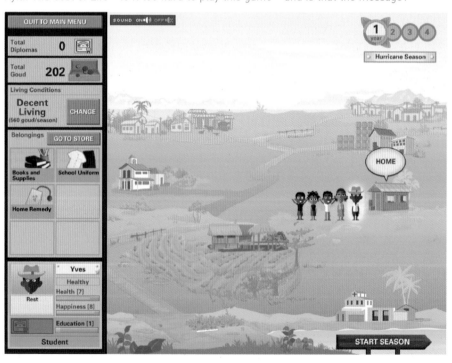

Gamelab, who collaborated in creating Ayiti: The Cost of Life, admits that the game is hard. 'The economies of the game are balanced with such guile that at first the game seems unbeatable', says the company. The challenge the designers faced was to create a game that realistically portrayed the straits of living under grinding poverty – but which was still satisfying to play. Their aim was to encourage people to play repeatedly, because each game would 'expose to the player most of the subtleties of the relationships between the different underlying economies.' Thus the message isn't that 'it's impossible to survive life in Haiti' – clearly that's not true. They just have to hope that the frustration of failure will pique people to keep trying in the heart-rending battle to keep Jean and Marie, and their children,

Patrick, Jacqueline and Yves, alive. If you want to find out more – take your involvement further – then there's information on the site about a discussion forum, or lesson plans for using in school.

Ian Bogost believes there is some power in the idea of an unwinnable game. 'When we aren't victorious it draws attention to the game and its subject matter, because it's surprising.' But a game that's just too hard to play may be counterproductive – Bogost finds it 'a precious design technique. It may be worse than having a straight-up unwinnable game.'

Or players may interpret a hard game differently to the way the creators intended. Madrid was released following the bombings at rail stations in the city on 11 March 2004, in which 191 people died. To mark the tragedy, Uruguayan-based company Newsgaming produced Madrid, only 2 days after the bombings. The game shows a mass of individuals holding candles, and wearing t-shirts emblazoned with Madrid and names of other cities affected by recent violence. By clicking on the flames, you make them burn brighter; a homage to the memory of those affected.

The effect is simple and moving, causing you to take time out just to think on what happened: a kind of 2 minutes' silent activity in a screamingly busy world. People playing using a laptop and glidepoint, however, discerned another layer of meaning. 'If you played Madrid with a trackpad it was very difficult to play fast enough, mechanically', explains Ian Bogost. 'So in some of the online discussions, people said "We're mourning and it's a never-ending process". That was a different reaction to the one you experience if you do complete the game.'

The power to provoke contrasting reactions is part of the power of persuasive games. But sometimes people question whether a situation is suitable to be turned into a game at all. See the section 'Fair Game?' for a discussion of the controversial game Darfur is Dying.

Does it matter if people get the 'wrong' idea about the meaning of a game? To some in the gaming community, it seems not. A game is 'art', so people can make of it what they will – and online message boards reveal an often-sophisticated dialogue about a game's interpretation (see the box 'A Hard Game for a Hard Life').

A Hard Game for a Hard Life

What's the sign of a successful persuasive game? Perhaps if it generates a useful discussion? Here's the involved debate about Ayiti: The Cost of Life on one message board.

'"An ok life" is the best I've managed, with 10 diplomas, good living conditions, and pretty high health and happiness for all of them . . . Frankly, I can't see how to get to excellent living or buy a new house or anything without some massive streak of luck – the best success I've had is always when the community center comes up quickly.'

Posted by: Valarauka   **7 November 2006 11:03 a.m.**

'I managed to end with 7–9 diplomas, $1000+, about 4 times so far (about half the games I played). Most of the advice found above is good, except that in my experience, you should only buy the books on turn 1 – the books have immediate effect, so you can test if they do anything, and other than on turn 1 they rarely ever do anything. How successful you'll be really depends a lot on luck, which I guess is also part of the message of the game. It doesn't matter how much you prioritize education and health if there aren't enough jobs available out there for your family to eat.'

Posted by: Eytan Zweig   **8 November 2006 2:03 a.m.**

'long time player . . . just posting a comment now . . . doesn't anyone else find this game really depressing? everyone dies of cholera and the underlying message seems to be that those in the poverty class are hopeless. i may be taking this game too seriously but its kinda scary'

Posted by: ex.infernis66   **27 March 2007 1:56 a.m.**

'@ex.infernis: Not at all true. I've had a few very successful families. I think the underlying message is that educated people can always get ahead. Read some of the walkthroughs and you should be able to cure your depression.'

Posted by: Evilwumpus   **13 April**

Fair Game?

Darfur is Dying is a game made by students at the University of Southern California to highlight the plight of people trapped in camps in Sudan. To play the game, you choose one of the child characters and set off across the desert to collect water, hiding every few seconds to avoid the Janjaweed militia whose trucks speed across the terrain. Playing the game late at night, with harrowing BBC News headlines playing out in another window on my computer, I found it to be a moving experience. So would someone who lives in Africa and deals with humanitarian situations every day find it a successful piece of communication? Laurie Nason is a pilot based in Kampala, Uganda. He works for Mission Aviation Fellowship, a Christian aid agency that flies relief to remote areas in Africa and elsewhere. He emailed me his thoughts as he was waiting for the game to load.

'Hi there,

I am waiting for your game to load on the slooooowwwww network connection here but already I have a few thoughts.

16% loaded . . .

I wonder if having a computer game trivialises the problems facing those people. Now, while I have not been to Darfur, we have had a similar situation here in Uganda where people have been forced from their own homes so I know only a little bit about what kind of situation they are living in. The thing about the north of Uganda is that there is some sort of peace right now between the rebels and the government while they have talks in Sudan over the matter – but even so, the people are still too scared to return to their homes. The particular camp I have in mind still has 5000 people living there.

52% loaded . . .

Also, I think that when people (actually me) play computer games it is some kind of escape from reality and so if I played something that was based on reality, I would probably have trouble realising that it is based on reality and on real people's lives and the decisions I took in the game, if taken in real life would or could lead to many people dying. I wouldn't want to have to make that decision in reality.

On the other hand, there may be some people who are able to realise the gravity of the situation (99% loaded . . .) and for the game to impact them for good.

OK enough for now – ran out of time to do much of the game – will try later . . .'

This response revealed much about the sensitive cultural and social issues that 'persuasive' games must negotiate. Laurie, more well-informed than most about issues affecting east Africa, felt uneasy about whether a game would capture the real tragedy experienced by people living in refugee camps.

He's also unsure about whether it's right to base a game on such a situation at all. He baulks at the idea that his decisions in the game should be a facsimile of real-life actions that could lead to real people dying.

Of course, this game is not intended to be fun. Like other persuasive games, Darfur is Dying makes the proposal that a game is a valid form for cultural criticism. Through its power of interpretation a game may be able to help us process, and therefore respond more adequately, to a humanitarian crisis. Had he got to play the game, Laurie might have been persuaded that other players would find it a convincing experience, raising awareness of the problems in Darfur, and perhaps leading to some kind of action to help.

But what strikes me about this particular example is the fact that Laurie *didn't* get to play the game at all. He is an ex-pat and well-off by Ugandan standards, yet he couldn't easily access the game. His 256k modem, although well-specced for the African infrastructure, would not load it fast enough for him to play in the time he had available.

A free game like this (actually sponsored by Reebok and MTVu, the US college-oriented TV network) is ostensibly 'available' to anyone who wants it. But, lacking the technology, not all are enfranchised to access it in practical terms. Does it matter if people living in Africa can't access a persuasive game made about an issue close-to-home? The game may still be successful in raising awareness among less well-informed people further away. But in itself, the issue speaks volumes about the have and have nots; those inside and outside the contemporary realm of political debate and influence.

Games to Save the Planet

Messages about how to save the planet don't seem to be getting any more exciting. Whether or not we're already aboard the bandwagon, we're bombarded with admonitions to 'stop doing that', 'switch that off' and 'don't use it all up'. It sometimes seems like a licence to stop people from having fun (or developing too much nasty technology to haul themselves out of poverty). How on earth could this kind of content become a must-play game?

It might sound like a challenge, but games about tackling climate change are proliferating. Starbucks have bolstered their eco-credentials with the online Planet Green Game made in collaboration with the US arm of Green Cross International (an organization founded in 1992 by Mikhail Gorbachev after the Rio Earth Summit). The game lets you explore a town by skateboard, on foot, by bike or different types of car, taking game-challenges on the way that introduce different green energy concepts. You can, of course, visit the local in-game Starbucks to write to the CEO, vote on your top-priority issues and . . . learn more about Starbucks.

It's quite fun and easy to play – a bit too easy in some ways – although it lacks an addictive quality (the music's nice). But does it communicate a strong message? The answer probably depends on your existing preconceptions about the messenger. Do you find Starbucks a convincing climate change campaigner? Does a global business have a right to tell you how to go greener, or only to tell us about how it is going greener itself? See the box 'Greenwashing', to see just how cynical one can be – or possibly ought to be.

Greenwashing?

Planet Green Game is all about how we can all contribute to saving the planet. Through our choices, we can help or hinder efforts to reduce emissions and keep the Earth in working order for longer.

While I was researching this chapter I asked my game-playing husband to try Planet Green Game and tell me what he thought. He soon grasped the game's fundamentals and reported back on how it all worked: some parts much better than others. But my response to the game had already been coloured, I think, by this fact: in the compact London borough where we used to live, there were three branches of Starbucks within spitting distance of each other. And for me, the idea that Starbucks cared about the planet's future was derailed by its part in the wasteful excess that often accompanies commercial success.

Here is our conversation, reproduced from our instant messenger logs.

YCY: Have played 'Planet Green Game'

me: do you love Starbucks now?

YCY: there are 6 primary objectives and 10 bonuses. i hv just made myself drive all over town looking for the bonuses

YCY: each bonus pops up a 50-100 panel eco-fact

YCY: i have found 9 of 10

me: do you score extra?

YCY: there is a Main eco-score – i dunno if bonuses increase that score

me: ok

YCY: it does decrease it that you have to fuel up a second time

YCY: from all the extra driving

me: right!

me: what are main objectives?

YCY: to visit 6 locations on the map: service station, house, school, building supply, city hall and city park

YCY: at each location you have a 'scoreable' challenge - which is different at each location

YCY: only one subgame is a bit ineffectual, which is the MPG game at the service station

YCY: truly underwhelming driving 'simulation'

me: haha

YCY: there is also a cinema with 8 short films abt eco

YCY: i watched 10 seconds of one.

YCY: my eco-bar appears to be at 100% - i guess i can stop now. . . . but i wonder where that last bonus is

me: so you don't know whether you have finished?

YCY: i have finished the primary objectives and my eco-bar is maximum

YCY: but one bonus remains uncollected

YCY: although i think i hv driven on every street in town now.

me: what do you feel was the main message?

YCY: 'you can make a difference'

me: that's interesting

YCY: hv got that last bonus now

YCY: on the exit splash screen it tells me i got 7900 out of 10000 possible points

me: seems like you should have got more?

me: didn't buy enough mocha lattes *tsk*

YCY: starbucks only features very incidentally

YCY: i got 'expert' rating – and a badge graphic for achieving that

me: sooper dooper!

me: free muffin?

YCY: ha no

YCY: from the link at the end of the game

'We can successfully tackle climate change by advocating for action on all levels:'

YCY: there seems to be a split in persuasive games that say 'you can make a difference' and those that say 'you can't'

YCY: even on the same topic.

me: less globalisation. smaller companies. an end to cultural imperialism

me: oh no! Starbucks must die!

YCY: ha

YCY: or at least decentralise itself

Sometimes, the relationship between commerce and campaigning is more subtle. A particularly nifty climate change game is Turn It All Off from 1E, a company that sells corporate energy-saving tools. 'Ten years ago no one used to turn off their computers. And the latest research shows that IT managers are still saying "don't turn the computers off" so that they can get automatic updates. We've got to keep going with the message', says 1E's CEO Sumir Karayi. 1E supply a product called NightWatchman which turns off banks of office computers safely and remotely overnight, waking them up only briefly to receive all-important patches and updates. Now they've personified the product with a game in which you have to switch off devices all over a typical office.

Nothing is made too blatant or harrying in this game – which makes it all the more memorable. Before you start playing, you have the option to see some sobering stats: £150 million a year is wasted because businesses leave computers on; five PCs use the same amount of energy as an electric heater and so on. Then the NightWatchman (embodied as a friendly mustachioed man) introduces you to the game, in which you tootle around an office switching off appliances, pursued by a troll who's determined to switch everything back on. If you get to level 2, you're awarded a larger office to take care of – but look out for the naughty photocopier. It's all good fun with enough challenge and charm to make you play over and over again. 'Though we make serious products, this game made the message much clearer', says Sumir.

Another green game to launch recently is Operation: Climate Control by Oxfordshire company Red Redemption. See the box 'Taking the Climate Challenge', to find out about the decisions they made.

Turn It All Off is a tongue-in-cheek race to switch off energy-hungry office equipment, made by 1E.

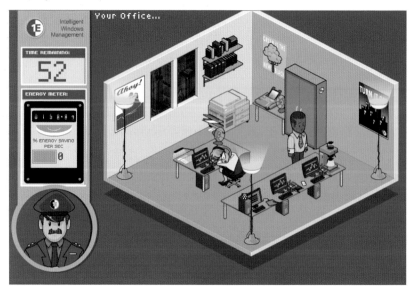

Taking the Climate Challenge

Gobion and Hannah Rowlands run Red Redemption, a company with growing experience in creating games that tackle green issues. I talked to them about the thinking behind their latest game Operation: Climate Control, funded by the UK government.

Why do you think games are good for putting across messages like this?

Hannah I think games are a great way of communicating important messages, especially potentially complicated ones, like climate change. The player can take their own time to explore the issues, and, if the game is designed well, can come to their own conclusions rather than be force-fed an opinion. And games can reach markets that more traditional media or learning tools do not reach, particularly the younger age groups.

Gobion Games are excellent at using simple mechanics to model and communicate understanding about complex issues. They are also well placed to make use of sub-conscious learning techniques, engaging the player with the game world – it's a natural and fun way of learning.

What did your research show about games and communicating climate change?

Hannah I surveyed 142 people about the effectiveness of games to communicate climate change issues, using one of our previous games as a case study (Climate Challenge). I found that the game did help people to feel more positive about their personal role in tackling climate change. Most people learned something – like what biomass is. There was an issue about trust in the information embodied in the game which would have to be addressed in future games. But most people enjoyed the game.

How did you bring this experience in to Operation: Climate Control?

Hannah   The key difference between Climate Challenge and Operation: Climate Control was the target audience, so we adapted what we'd learned and made it more relevant for a teenage audience. We also had to make it suitable for playing in a short time, for the classroom. There's also more of an element of comparison with other players instead of getting one player to try loads of strategies themselves. We also wanted to give a more holistic view of climate change, and to show that there is a scientific consensus.

Do you see Operation: Climate Control as being part of a particular genre of games?

Gobion   We see Operation: Climate Control as "Smart" games, rather than "Serious Games" which are traditionally associated with the military. Smart games should make people think. They can be used to help make positive change aspirational, because they can communicate vastly complex issues in a simple way that everyone can get to grips with.

Operation Climate Control doesn't force-feed players, but lets them come to their own conclusions.

Would You Do Something If a Game Told You To?

It's inescapable that all games are steeped in a cultural context that is going to carry a perspective – and nowhere is this more obvious than in a game that recreates military action. In August 2007, the Lebanese Shiite group Hezbollah released a computer game based on the 34-day war that erupted with Israel in summer 2006. 'This game presents the culture of the resistance to children: that occupation must be resisted and that land and the nation must be guarded', a Hezbollah spokesman told Reuters. The game, which puts players in the frontline, attacking Israeli tanks and launching missiles, was unveiled with fanfare – and a display of Israeli tanks damaged during the conflict – in south Beirut.

'There's a handful of games produced in the Middle East, for example by Hezbollah', Ian Bogost told me. Hezbollah is considered a terrorist group in the USA and the UK, although others see it as a legitimate resistance force. 'Many in the West look with revulsion on these games. But then our industries release games about Delta Force Invasions', says Ian.

America's Army (AA) is a game produced by the US military as a recruitment tool. Based on the same technology as the first-person shooter game Unreal, it is a tactical first-person multiplayer shooter game and has been an enormous communications success. Since its launch in 2002, the game has been downloaded 40 million times, and in 2007 the game's makers also announced the launch of a coin-operated arcade version. Although AA can't be proven to have caused an upturn in military recruitment, 19% of recruits in 2003 said they'd played the game. 'The game has exceeded all expectations in placing Soldiering front and center within popular culture and showcasing the roles training, teamwork and technology play in the Army', read a 2002 report from the army's Game Leadership Team.

To visit the game website is to enter a world where you're not sure what's real and what isn't. The game itself (in its edition for the Xbox) is introduced by a trailer, Rise of a Soldier, which proclaims that 'Great soldiers aren't born. They're made.' The animation is realistic, introducing the idea of a soldier completing basic military training before going into battle – a conceit that allows new players to complete training missions before launching into multiplayer mode. But elsewhere on the site are 'Real Heroes': profiles of US Army soldiers with descriptions of their achievements in the arena of war. Strangely, though, they are depicted in the same game-style graphics as the character in the trailer. This seems uncomfortable: are they real-life survivors of conflict, or pixel soldiers who'll always come back from screen-based war?

As you might expect, there's been debate over the realism of the game itself. Weaponry is authentic, but nobody gets graphically shredded when they're hit. If your compatriots die, they'll die in a neat, tidy kind of way. There's little in the way of discussion as to the mental state of the soldiers as they train for battle. In a subtle piece of programming, players on both teams see themselves dressed as US soldiers and the opposing team dressed as foreign militia. But this is all classic manoeuvring in the genre of 'media with a mission': you put in what you want to show, and you leave the rest out. After all, this is a game, not a simulation.

So it is a good game? Some gamers see it in the same light as any first-person shooter. Others find some of the gameplay somewhat dull – after all, an assault course that you negotiate by pressing the 'c' key is inevitably less engaging than the real thing. Ultimately the aim of the game is to nurture a positive, unquestioning attitude towards the US Army, and all the game designers' choices seem to support that.

Propaganda Gone Wrong

Games make good persuasive tools – especially when their subject matter meshes with prevailing game technology. But in one case at least, fiction outran reality in reports that malign forces were using games for propaganda. In May 2006, a technology consultant appeared before a US Intelligence Committee to explain how terrorists were increasingly using the Internet for the purposes of propaganda and recruitment. 'Nowhere is this more evidence than in the computer games that they're using as they target the youth', he told the committee, showing a video that he had downloaded from an insurgent website. The video, he claimed, was footage from a game created to condition players to kill coalition soldiers. It showed animated combat between insurgents and US troops, with the opening lines '*I was just a boy when the infidels came to my village in Blackhawk helicopters*'. In grave tones, the consultant told the assembled company: 'What we have seen is that any video game that comes out . . . [al Qaeda will] modify it and change the game for their needs'.

Trouble was, the consultant was completely wrong about the example he'd chosen. Rather than being an edition of Battlefield 2 specially modified by insurgents to warp young minds, the footage actually came from an add-on module to the game available in any US games shop. The opening lines, people spotted, actually came from a 2004 spoof film by the creators of *South Park*, called *Team America: World Police*. And the person who had put it all together was a fan of Battlefield 2 living in Holland, who had made his video using the in-game battle recorder. He didn't intend his creation to have any particular message. 'The video was just for fun. It was a fan-film made by me', he told website Gamepolitic.

This is the *idea* of propaganda games being used as propaganda! And to have a game intended 'just for fun' used so rashly in such a high-stakes environment shocked Gonzalo Frasca, an expert in persuasive gaming. He uncovered the story over a number of days, growing increasingly incredulous at what he was finding. 'If you pay big money to consultants, they should do their job right or you should get new consultants. This is not about a meteorologist who predicted sunshine for the weekend and ruined your barbecue', he wrote.

The incident illustrates the significance in persuasive gaming of knowing who's made a game – and what they're really trying to do with it: something rarely, if ever, asked of ordinary computer games.

What Would You Buy If a Computer Game Told You To? Advergames

One of the earliest links between games and advertising appeared in 1978 when Fuji released a Coca Cola-customized version of the TV controller used for Pong. The knobs were Coke-bottle tops and the case was coloured the characteristic Coca-Cola red.

Much has changed since then. Today, advertising needn't mean a full-page ad in the newspaper or a slot on prime-time television. Advertising now appears in many big-ticket games, on a virtual billboard or as sponsor advertising on a racing car. And viral games – distributed between gamers themselves – have proven effective at spreading to thousands of machines.

Advertising often leads the way in new media, and – before the dotcom crash set them back somewhat – was starting to ride a wave of innovation in games technology. 'The advertising agencies used to tout their abilities by sending out holiday cards as a showcase', says Ian Bogost. One such game was Snowball Fight, which made its appearance at Christmas in the office in which I worked back in 2000. I remember it arriving on one person's machine, and in no time, being everywhere, with that mysterious capacity of viral games spread from friend to friend. We red teamsters spent quite some time pounding the green team with snowballs until their little hats and snowboots came off and we could go to the next level of mindless mayhem.

And mindless it apparently was. I had no recollection of any message about the game, which was apparently made by a major advertising and brand-marketing firm Nicholson New York. Nonetheless, 'It was a cute experience', says Ian, 'and advertising still has this obsession with viral spread. But that game didn't necessarily carry with it the message that its makers intended to convey.'

Five years later, and the agencies were back online. In 2005, Agency.com revived Snowball Fight with a clever new twist. Instead of playing anonymous red- and green-clothed characters, the game now invited you to take the role of the agency or the client, each shown in appropriate caricature guise. The ensuing snowthrow took place against a backdrop of cities in which you would find offices of Agency.com. A stronger message? Certainly – you took away a sense that this group knew what they were doing in the world of slick digital interactives. And in a climate of increasingly knowing media communications, the tongue-in-cheek message worked, too, satirizing the ongoing creative struggle between client and agency.

Other corporate games don't take such a clever approach. On Siemens' website you can play a game called Spinopolis in which you answer quiz questions to gain features for a swanky new version of Berlin, Los Angeles or Shanghai. In one round, the game poses a question about what a car's 'odometer' measures. The answer came with a loosely related corporate factoid: 'Siemens' (sic) makes miniature automotive lights and you can find them utilized in 50% of the cars in the US'. I thus earned a transportation system for New Shanghai. By answering 20-or-so more intriguingly US-centric questions about the world and its development of technology ('which of these US presidents was the first to travel by plane?'), I added a new medical centre, energy system (unspecified), 3G-enabled office block and communication network. *Solutions for sustainable urban development* was the main article on the Siemens corporate website, which you were invited to visit at the end of the game. I could see why they had included a button on the cityscape 'Too busy to finish? Click here'. The message they hoped I would take away – that Siemens technology is building the world of tomorrow – was delivered, but without a flourish. This game is intended to be viral – but I can't see it spreading very far or fast.

Coke Pong: an early example of an advergame?

PowerPamplona is a different proposition entirely. With edgy graphics, and to a soundtrack of Spanish drums, you're drawn in to a bull-chase through the streets of Pamplona, Spain. Once you complete an initial level (by escaping the bull through an upper-floor window) you're into the first playoff of an international tournament. I unfortunately perished as I tried to jump over barrels to escape a comedy barmaid plying me with drink, so I don't know what the other levels are. But it was fun. The product? Sure deodorant. I now think of the brand as more sophisticated and appealing than before – even though I'm hardly the prime audience for a men's toiletry.

PowerPamplona negotiates a key tension between normal adverts and advergames. Adverts are usually designed to be easily consumed and accessed – whereas the nature of a game is to obstruct your progress and challenge you. This game keeps you playing, while subtly reinforcing compelling messages about the brand's appeal.

Adverts are **usually designed** to be **easily consumed and accessed** – whereas the nature of a **game** is to **obstruct your progress** and **challenge you**

But along with the on-message games have come underground games that have come to be known as 'anti-advergames'. They spoil the party for corporate marketing departments, and keep the whole field interesting for consumers.

Do Persuasive Games Tell It Like It Is?

You might think that, in a game where you're calling the shots, you'd be in control. Sim games like SimCity, SimEarth, Civilization and some of the multiple-variable games we've discussed so far seem to put you in charge – that's why they're often called God games. 'What [God games] offer is the modelling of dynamic processes. Time can be sped up or slowed down at will, and interactions of data over time can be readily visualized', says Steven Poole in his book about the aesthetics and history of computer games, *Trigger Happy*. 'In this way, fiddling with the fiscal and monetary operators of SimCity for a couple of minutes and observing the results for the next accounting period provides a remarkably intuitive way to understand the fundamentals of balancing a budget in a capitalist state.' Like a bona fide simulation, the programmer can include as many variables as he or she can think of, create relationships between them ('if you double this variable, it'll cause this related variable to halve') and then sit back to see what happens.

That same power is embodied in sim games – you can try stuff out to see what happens. And it's a surprisingly powerful way of absorbing understanding. In *Everything Bad Is Good for You*, Steven Johnson describes introducing the game

Anti-advergame Disaffected! lampoons the customer service at a real-life printing chain in the US Copyright Persuasive Games.

SimCity to his 7-year-old nephew one rainy day. Johnson created a town and scrolled around it, pointing out landmarks and features as if it were a model train set. But after about an hour's play, as Johnson was trying to revive a rundown area of his proto-city, his nephew suddenly piped up 'I think we need to lower our industrial tax rates.' Don't forget, this chap was 7 years old.

Simulation games are certainly powerful. And for issues where there are many variables to juggle – running a country's budget, for example – it's a great way for game designers to show how one thing leads to another. But are you really 'in control' of a complex system modelled on a computer? Without seeing all the inner workings – everything the designer and programmer had to contend with in creating the game – aren't you at its whim? Steven Poole thinks so. In strong contrast to the hero-centric shoot-'em-up games in which the action of the player is paramount, Poole notices that he doesn't get the same vibe from a sim game. 'There seems to be a pernicious subterranean motive here: such games offer you a position of infinite power in order to whisper the argument that, as an individual in the world, you have none at all.'

Thinkers like Sherry Turkle worry that players of games like SimCity don't grasp the concept of 'critical play'. If you do well in the game, that must mean you're doing the right thing – right? Well – it depends on your point of view. Critics have pointed out that The Sims reinforces notions of consumer capitalism by rewarding greed. To make your characters happy, what do you do? Buy them some new stuff. Others argue that in its sheer devotion to gleaming new purchases the game is actually parodying modern consumerism. But do players see the difference?

Some sophisticated persuasive games – which can be remarkably difficult to play – deliberately tinker with the ideas of games that can't be won. Disaffected!, a game about a photocopying shop, puts the player into the role of an employee, dealing with customer orders and complaints. But it's a parody – intended to lampoon the terrible service received by many customers at a real-life printing chain in the USA. So as you play, other employees move paperwork around at random so you can't find it; your character starts moving its arms in the opposite direction to your mouse movements; orders are completed, only for customers to find they've been done wrongly. The game forcefully communicates the idea that going to this chain of shops will be a baffling experience, with the shop workers apparently following rules designed to frustrate you: frustration in the game tells you that you're not likely to enjoy visiting the shop in real life.

The game **forcefully** communicates the **idea** that going to this **chain** of shops will be **a baffling experience**

The Museum Is the Message

In other realms, it's felt to be crucial that games put over the intended message. Eric Newton helped develop the Newseum, the world's first museum dedicated to the news industry, in Washington DC, which opened in 1997. They were seeking to spread a message, as he told me: 'We very strongly wanted to find out if was possible to teach people of all ages some of the most fundamental values of our society – freedom of expression, as we embody in the First Amendment and diversity of information in the press.' The aim went beyond mere 'learning' – there was an agenda to put across, too. How best to do this, reaching out to a non-specialist audience of families and school groups? 'It had to be fun and interesting – so we decided to develop interactive games', Eric said.

The Newseum opened with a suite of computer games including Be a Reporter, Be an Editor, Be a Photographer and Interview a Journalist. These were branching games that allowed multiple pathways 'so within the game you could embed a tremendous amount of material, which we researched from real journalists and real news material', Newton says, himself an award-winning former newspaper editor. And how were the games received? 'Usually school kids are called "Drano" in museums – because they clear everyone else out of the way like the corrosive drain-cleaning chemical. We didn't want that – we wanted them to stop and do things.' And that was what happened. Along with the kids came the adult visitors. 'We didn't focus on making the games too simple or hard, just fun. You can't make things too fun.'

So, now for the 64-thousand-dollar question. Did visitors get the message? Newton, now Director of Journalism Initiatives at the non-profit Knight Foundation in Miami, is positive they did. 'People – at least news museum visitors – are naturally curious and you don't have to hit them over the head. In the gaming environment people picked up a lot of subtlety and nuance. They really did learn the basic principles of journalism and ethics. As well as the real fundamental point – freedom of expression is necessary and you need to consume news from more than one source to find out what's really going on.' You could also argue that the element of choice in the game reinforced the message about personal action having significance.

❮❮ People **picked up** a lot of **subtlety** and **nuance**. They **really** did learn the **basic principles of journalism** and ethics **❯❯**

In 2006, the Copenhagen-based company Serious Games Interactive released an ambitious journalism-based game. Global Conflicts: Palestine puts you in the shoes of a freelance reporter arriving in Israel, and trying to stay neutral while searching for a story. At the time the Newseum opened, Newton says they didn't classify the games they were developing as 'serious' or 'persuasive': games with an overt message were in their infancy.

For museums today, the practice is more familiar. The Science Museum in London takes a message-based approach to all its new galleries and exhibitions, developing hierarchical levels of information that build together to support top-level messages. Those messages may be factual information, or – more in keeping with the notion of games as having procedural rhetoric – they are ideas about how things work, socially, morally, scientifically, culturally.

Global Conflicts: Palestine puts you in the role of a journalist and challenges you to weigh up evidence and write a news story.

Spiral worked with the Science Museum on message-based games for Energy: Fuelling the Future including Making Energy Useful (*top left and right*, a Dance Dance Revolution-inspired game in which you match energy sources to technologies – using your feet) and Smart Arse (*bottom left*, a game that features an annoying know-it-all boy with multiple fathers who goes around the house telling them all how to save energy). For Nuclear Waste: Can You Handle It? Spiral managed to get everyone playing a really quite serious arcade-type game called Nukeman (*bottom right*).

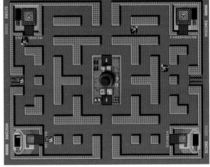

Space Invaders was one of Simon's early influences. 'In the early '80s we used to sit down in the pub at lunchtime and play tabletop computer games: I don't think we realised at the time that we were witnessing a new medium and subculture being born.'

Digital interactives and games play an important role in communicating these messages. Simon Lucas is a designer at creative company Spiral Productions who has worked with the Science Museum on dozens of games and screen-based toys that aim to get the message across. 'I think that what works about the Science Museum's approach is the way in which they develop a clear methodology for developing and commissioning exhibits. They could write great briefs', Simon told me. 'This gave us – the developers – the permission and freedom to interpret ideas within a well-defined framework.'

That freedom has allowed Lucas and partners to play around with play. 'The visual gag is very important', he tells me. 'Laughter is important when dealing with communicating with children and adults. If you can make people laugh and play with their expectations of what they're going to get, then that opens a window in people's minds through which you can reach them.'

❝ If you can make people **laugh** and **play** with their expectations of what they're **going to get,** then that **opens a window** in people's minds **❞**

'We're trying out something new for Tate Modern', Simon tells me. 'They wanted to talk about different artists in some depth, and we knew it might get very information-heavy, with complex ideas. We proposed mixing the information with gameplay, drawing in cartoons and using the concept of Wario games that only last a few seconds.' Each game communicates a feeling about the artist and how each one worked. 'It's completely pointless in terms of a specific educational content, but what they do is to create a memorable experience. There's something about Wario that's very irreverent: it appeals to me – it makes me laugh and draws on a long history of computer gaming and subversive daftness.'

❝ But what they do is to **create a memorable experience.** There's **something** about Wario that's **very irreverent ❞**

Simon believes it's important that games with a message retain subtlety, even if they're of the 'quick hit' variety. 'It's a good idea to focus on the big ideas that the public come away with', he says.

Tate Modern is using Spiral's take on Wario games to get across messages about modern artists. As part of the Tate's Learning Zone, the exhibits use gameplay to enhance learning, helping information reach its audience.

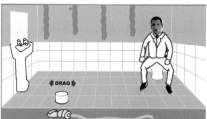

Conclusion

To Simon Lucas, hitting people over the head with a message that's too obvious seems counterproductive. 'I don't like hammering a message home', he says. 'If you push points at people, it's like an assault. I prefer things I don't quite understand; they send me back to think more.'

And that's the message I've taken away from my tour of persuasive games. Games are powerful – yes – and we've a lot further to go in exploring their full scope as a persuasive tool. They can get us to think, engage and experiment in ways we might not with other media. We can put ourselves into the roles of different characters and see how life works for them: whether they're a refugee or an insurgent.

But for games to be truly mind-changing, their makers need to understand where the game ends and the diatribe begins. Nobody's convinced by a so-called game that's just an excuse for spouting corporate jargon, or crow-barring in factoids. The best games are those that, at least in their appearance, allow the player to make up their own mind about the message, the product, the party, the brand. By putting that responsibility into the player's hands, the designers lose control – but the game gains enormous power.

And as game consumers, perhaps we need to ask harder questions about who's making games and why. Blockbuster games have implicit messages just as persuasive games do – and we need a more sophisticated discussion of those messages and their impact. Although makers of persuasive games love to discuss their work, big games companies are notoriously tight-lipped about the motivations behind their products. Only when game-players start asking more searching questions will games start getting the cultural airtime they deserve.

8 Can Computer Games Change Your Future?

Who will decide how computer games develop in the future? The scientists who can see the physical ways in which games can change us? The social scientists who are watching games trigger the growth of new kinds of communities and relationships? The industry, with some of the brightest programmers and designers in its fold? The engineers and entrepreneurs who create new technologies and bring them to a consumer audience? Or the artists, whose new ideas have the potential to change the way we think about computer games altogether?

Whoever wields majority power – just look at what they could do with it. This book so far has examined the power of computer games in changing how we live, and established that we're coming into a time when computer games will be a convincing cultural force. They can help us reflect on the world, train us in new skills; exercise and rehabilitate our bodies, stretch our minds in new directions, reveal truths about our behaviour and that of others, campaign to change the things we care about, rev us up or calm us down, change our worlds.

"Do you play computer games?" A recent BBC survey showed a 100% positive response from 6- to 10-year-olds

But many of us aren't playing games. The numbers of gamers and people who are buying new technologies are growing – yes. But not nearly as many of us play games as watch television or read books. The revolution's already here among the young: a recent BBC survey showed a 100% positive response from 6- to 10-year-olds, when asked 'Do you play computer games?' When will we develop the same expectation that 35-year-old women will play games? Or 92-year-old men?

How will future games play with reality?

COURTESY OF VIENNA UNIVERSITY OF TECHNOLOGY

In this final brief chapter, I'll look at some of the biggest barriers that keep games from reaching into lives otherwise saturated with media. As part of this I'll show some of the ideas and technologies that might appear in the next generation of games and game technology, and how that might make the benefits of games more widely available. I'll also look at what proposals people made when I asked 'What would be your ideal game of the future?' – and whether the industry might be able to respond.

Games Aren't Immersive Enough

The predominant 'wish' among people who answered my survey was a more realistic experience in games. This could be a significant help in climbing the 'learning curve' in games and getting on with the action, whether it's for entertainment, learning, health or social interaction. For some people this meant new technology that they could wear and use: Michael, 23, hankered after 'a return to true characterization, meshed with the next-generation of immersive input. Who knows what that is – I just know I can't wait to play it'. Jack, 16, mentioned 'a full body suit so you could move as the character'. A 20-year-old survey respondent wanted 'a virtual role playing game. Like in films, with a mask, hat and hand movements to control the game, so you feel like you're really in it.'

Emotiv is developing a new wireless headset that reads your brainwaves and will enable more natural interaction with computer-generated worlds. Nam Do, CEO, explained his vision. 'The interactivities in the virtual world of today are seriously lacking expression and emotion', he told me. 'We can definitely see Emotiv contributing a big part in this field by allowing people to express themselves more freely and intuitively in the future.'

The 16-sensor system works by using electroencephalography (EEG) to measure electrical activity in the brain. Emotiv detects three kinds of signals, as Nam

Emotiv allows you to control the game just by thinking.

explains: '*Expressiv* detects a set of facial expressions, *Affectiv* is designed for emotions and *Cognitiv* differentiates between thoughts and cognitive intents'. By feeding these high-resolution EEG signals to some specially designed algorithms, they can then generate an 'image' of the brain in multi-dimensional space for different thoughts, emotions and expressions.

It's the first time, according to Nam, that technology has allowed people and machines to communicate so naturally. 'Machines now are able to understand not only your conscious intents but can also read expressions and sense how you feel about what you're seeing and hearing', he said.

How does the kit make your gaming experience immersive? Nam says that the *Expressiv* gives players realistic control over their avatar's facial expression, while the *Affectiv* is how the game understands whether you're bored, excited, calm or frustrated. This should mean the game can adjust to suit your mood and ability.

Cognitiv gives gamers control over their movement and actions in the game – just by thinking about them. Game developers are now working with the three tools to integrate them into forthcoming games.

Many survey respondents talked about wanting games that were immersive and extremely natural. One female gamer in her forties said she'd like 'having avatars exactly like yourself so you could experience things that you will never get to do in real life', while another tellingly asked for 'virtual reality with lots of activities and no technical issues.' A 37-year-old male gamer understandably wanted 'the fun of playing god, realistic experiences without actual risk of death or other undesirable consequences.'

NeuroSky Inc, a San Jose, California company, believes that its technology will transform the casual and serious game landscape because it's easy to use and affordable to the mass gaming market (that's us).

NeuroSky has created a brainwave-reading device that is able to pick up your brainwaves and muscle movements on your face with a single, dry sensor headset. ThinkGear's mind-sensing capabilities will also enable your avatar automatically to express how you feel in game worlds such as There, where there is already an expressive palette of emotion animations, but which does not yet respond auto-matically to your voice.

This neural technology can also tell if you're concentrating (sit up at the back), meditating, anxious or drowsy, with more capabilities on the horizon. Greg Hyver, the VP of Marketing at NeuroSky, believes that this technology will add greater realism into computer gameplay. For example, the need to concentrate when lining up a golf shot has been incorporated into a realistic golf game demo: 'Players have to pay attention to the shot. If they're not focusing, they dribble it or hook the ball', he said.

NeuroSky's single-sensor headset allows you to control virtual movement by the power of thought, and may reveal how our emotions peak during gameplay.

REPRINTED WITH PERMISSION FROM NEUROSKY

ThinkGear allows you to control virtual movement by the power of thought: 'We have a multiplayer game where you can lift and push objects using your mind', Greg said. 'There's a car in the middle of a room and it's very heavy. You can try to lift it by clearing your mind but you can't do it by yourself – you have to used combined mental strength with another player.'

Like Nam Do, Greg also believes the emotion-sensing capabilities could also be applied to how games are made. 'The current way to develop games is to design

Immersive, realistic and **player-focused games** – which **perhaps** enable tailored **learning** and **brain-training experiences** as well as simple entertainment – *may* be just a **thought** away

something, talk to a focus group or get them to play, survey them to see if they like it', he says. 'The next step is to get a real-time picture of how consumers are feeling by using EEG and biosensors to gauge player reactions during actual game-play, then adapt the game until a desired emotional response is achieved.' Games will self-adjust to the particular individual playing them, instead of being targeted at the focus group average. For example, if a particular scene is meant to elicit a relaxed mental state, but an individual gamer feels otherwise, then the game itself can try new approaches to soothe and relax them. Ultimately, this will make the gaming experience much more enjoyable and tailored to the individual. Immersive, realistic and player-focused games – which perhaps enable tailored learning and brain-training experiences as well as simple entertainment – *may* be just a thought away.

Games Should Engage Our Emotions More

Lots of people who replied to the survey asked for games that would make them feel they were in the middle of the action. Mark, 33, asked for a game 'in which I actually feel I am there. Even the great leaps in advancement from say Xbox to 360 don't grab me that much'. Rachid, 28, wanted 'a VR game where you are totally immersed in the game itself.' Daisy, 9, showed that sight and sound are not all that's involved in making an experience 'real', asking for 'a game where you can smell whatever you are cooking.'

One way to achieve immersion is through new display technology, for sure. But how about if you could achieve a better 'fit' between game and gamer by testing its emotional impact before it went to market? We've seen that games can benefit your self-esteem (see Chapter 1, 'Can Computer Games Affect Your Health?') – so how can we track players' emotional state as they play?

Jon Sykes is so interested in how we relate emotionally to computer games, he's created a whole lab to keep track of gamers' responses. At Glasgow Caledonian University, eMotion is a state-of-the-art set-up that includes gadgets to track every last detail of your gameplay experience.

'There are a lot of labs that try to gauge people's responses to computer games by measuring the change in conductivity over the skin's surface as you're playing' Jon told me. 'The theory is that changes in perspiration caused by stress affect the conductivity. But the problem is that you're tethered to the equipment – it's not naturalistic. We try to make our data ecologically valid by monitoring people in a normal setting.'

This 'normal setting' is a realistic-looking living room – complete with a trendy picture of pebbles on the wall. The only odd thing is that there's a huge one-way window facing the sofa, which allows researchers to see what their volunteers are up to. Remote-control cameras capture every movement, smile and grimace, and all the video data is digitised and annotated in real-time. 'We've put an eye-tracker under the monitor the gamer uses', Jon says. 'It lets us see what the player's looking at, but also how dilated their pupils are.' Pupil dilation might mean you're emotionally or even sexually aroused – there really are no secrets in here.

❝❝ **Pupil dilation** might mean you're **emotionally** or even **sexually aroused** – there really are **no secrets** in here ❞❞

eMotion has other subtle ways of monitoring how your gaming experience is going. 'We've engineered a gamepad so that when you press the button, it gives us an analogue data signal that shows how hard you pressed it', explains Jon. More pressure on the buttons indicates greater arousal. The gamepad also contains accelerometers to record how much you wiggle it around during play.

But the most cunning sensor – in my opinion – is one that you definitely won't spot while you're in the lab. Jon describes how the team was commissioned to find out what was the scariest computer game. 'It's no good relying on verbal feedback – it's too subjective and people forget things.' How did the team tackle this problem objectively? No – not with a sensor that measures how much your hair is standing on end. They simply fitted a sensor under the cushion on which the players sat. 'We can give an objective measure of when people are literally sitting on the edge of their seat', Jon explains.

The team was **commissioned** to **find out** what was **the scariest computer game.** It's **no good** relying on **verbal feedback** – it's **too subjective** and people **forget things**

What happens to this slew of data that's captured? It's fed through to the hidden researchers, who can then graph the peaks and troughs of players' arousal and relate them to the events onscreen. They also look at the facial muscles to try to find out whether the arousal was due to excitement – a positive emotion – or frustration – a more negative one.

All the interest in emotional reactions to games is in order to take games to the next level of sophistication. Games in the future may be able to respond to your emotional levels dynamically, which would be helpful if you're distracted at a crucial emotional peak by the pizza man arriving. While other media would just have to pause and restart, future games may be able to re-play the emotional crescendo so that the gaming experience isn't ruined.

The eMotion lab contains hidden sensors and cameras to track a player's every reaction to the game he or she is playing.

Using the **street-based** driving **game Project Gotham,** she found that **people reported** the **most emotional experience,** plus a **reduction in tension and anxiety,** when they **played** while listening to their **own selected** music

Can Music Change Your Gaming Experience?

Ninety percent of gamers say that music is integral to their gaming experience, according to Gianna Cassidy's findings. At Glasgow Caledonian University she's studying how music changes the experience of a game – and her results so far show there's a strong influence on our enjoyment, performance and learning.

- In a study using the street-based driving game Project Gotham, she found that people reported the most emotional experience, plus a reduction in tension and anxiety, when they played while listening to their own selected music.
- But when Gianna used music that she had specially selected to be aggressive and fast, players were the least good at the game.

■ Seventy-one percent of players used self-chosen music, according to research. And they seem to do it to actively raise their level of excitement or to calm down and relax.

'Music really is a fundamental channel of communication. But we tend to ignore its important affective role', says Gianna. 'It helps the communication of game information to the player. It appears that music can help the player concentrate, stay calm and not get irritated. It was evidence from the research that listening to self-chosen music aided the players' learning curve.'

Games Should Get Us away from the Screen

Screen-based games are so passé. Well, that's how it seems from the numbers of researchers experimenting with computer-mediated games that take place in locations far removed from the standard living room. This could be a huge boost for anyone looking to use games to promote physical activity alongside problem-solving, whether for formal education or not. And it seems as though such games should be popular. In my survey, David, 38, was looking for a game 'which breaks down the barriers between different players of different ages. There's something disruptive about games on a screen. It just doesn't really work as a group activity'.

Rebecca, 27, hoped for something 'interactive, involving lots of people, in 3D', while Jake, 32 said 'I'd like to play a game in a room with 3D graphics on all the walls and where I could act out motions and the computer/console would detect these motions and translate them into game actions.' Although some labs are working on this kind of technology, we're still years away from anything as intuitive as *Star Trek*'s Holodeck.

What about leaving the indoors behind all together? Dutch company TNO Defense, Safety and Security is working on new technologies for 'the future soldier', including a communication and information module (CIM) that combines navigation tools with local maps and intelligence. Effectively, the CIM overlays location-specific information onto the real landscape using GPS to tells what's where.

To test how effective soldiers found the CIM, researchers developed a virtual city using the Unreal engine and mapped it to a real outdoor location. Soldiers had to try to locate an arms dealer, 25 of them using the CIM and the other half using standard techniques. 'The CIM significantly increased the soldiers' speed and effectiveness, but also their situational awareness', said Robert de Bruin. They also found that they could increase the reality of the situation by including more uncertainty: noises and extra people outside the soldiers' control.

Could this be the kind of game we would all play in the future? Artists' group Blast Theory has also been trying out these 'augmented reality' games, working in collaboration with the Mixed Reality lab at Nottingham University. Uncle Roy All Around You is a game played both online in a virtual city, and on the streets of a real city. The street players have to try to find Uncle Roy's office within an hour, using clues and information sent to them via a handheld computer. Online players can send messages to guide or misdirect them.

'With Uncle Roy All Around You we were playing with the boundary between games and everyday life', says artist Matt Adams. 'In the game you're not sure who else

Soldiers in the Netherlands explored a virtual city created using the Unreal engine. Researcher Robert de Bruin said 'Most soldiers had gaming experience and queued up enthusiastically to join in with the experiment. They took it seriously as soldiers, though.'

REPRINTED VERWIJS, C., BRUIN, R. DE VLIET, A.J. VAN (2007). AUTHORITY AND RESPONSIBILITY OF THE DISMOUNTED SOLDIER, PART B: IMPROVING THE SITUATIONAL AWARENESS USING THE SOLDIER DIGITAL ASSISTANT IN A SIMULATED ENVIRONMENT. REPORT TNO-DV 2007 A142, SOESTERBERG, THE NETHERLANDS: TNO DEFENSE, SECURITY AND SAFETY is playing; who else is an actor. You might mistake a passer-by for an actor, or go into a post office and say you're there for Uncle Roy. It's risky – and that's one of the reasons these games aren't more widespread.

But that is part of the message. As the game develops you're asked – when you finally get to Roy's office – whether you are willing to make a commitment to a stranger. You don't know whether it's a genuine question, but in fact if you do make the commitment, you're paired up with another player after the game. If one of you has a crisis during the next 12 months, the other one has to help pick up the pieces.

It's all about trust and community, and their limits. Our technology and mobile devices are always on – we're always connected, but how real are those links? Do we have a responsibility to each other in life, or in virtual space? These are precisely the questions raised by our lives online.

How **real** are **those** links? **Do we** have a **responsibility to each other** in **life,** or in **virtual space**?

And is it fun? Well, that's not really the point. 'Part of what we are doing is expanding the sense of possibility for what games might be', says Matt. 'I've been playing computer games since I was ten so I am in the first wave of people who have grown up with games as an integral part of our lives. There are more and more people who, like me, aren't satisfied with the blockbusters.'

Great fun is how I'd describe a game trialled by TNO, judged the most innovative game and grand prix winner at the International Mobile Gaming Awards in 2007.

Do we really know what's happening in the game Uncle Roy All Around You?

Triangler is a massive collaborative geometric outdoor mobile interactive game. Got that? Two 50-strong teams try to enclose enemy players within 150-metre equilateral triangles formed by three team members. Triangler uses advanced mobile location and communication services to enable team members to collaborate and trap the maximum number of enemy in their triangles – without being caught themselves. 'This technology could be used for large-scale training programmes for disaster workers', says inventor Oskar van Deventer. Lead developer Victor Klos added 'We're all already carrying around the next generation of smartphones with GPS – and this is what makes the game work.'

Triangler uses advanced **mobile location** and **communication services** to **enable** team members to **collaborate** and **trap the maximum number** of enemy in their **triangles**

Games Should Be More Diverse

One or two of the people who answered my survey came up with really quite . . . unusual ideas for new games. And there is now such a mass of creative people from diverse backgrounds getting interested in game-making that we can hope to see a much greater range of ideas emerging in game form than the current limited scope of most big-budget titles.

Barry, 37, said he'd like 'a morally ambiguous first person adventure set on a remote planet in which elaborate puzzles need to be completed in order to progress. And lots of shooting'. OK. And Steven, 40, thought 'an online shooter for 40+ year olds' would be good – but he specified he didn't want any of the ranks 'addressing other players as sir.' What a rebel. Phil, 35, came from left field with his game idea: 'managing an animal band and entering dance competitions with them'.

Triangler: a game in which you catch enemies in . . . a triangle.

Phil, 35, came from left field with his game **idea**: **"managing an animal band** and entering **dance competitions** with them"

Phil, it's your lucky day. The Mixed Reality Lab in Singapore has come up with a game that you can play with your animal friends. And it's been specifically designed for those times when you can't be with them, yet you still want to have a good old game of chase.

'I'm keen to use new media to produce positive feelings and interactions', Adrian David Cheok, lab director, told me. His team had previously worked on a project in which you could hug your pet over the Internet. 'We thought, wouldn't it be good if you could play a *game* remotely?' says. Normally, hamsters get their exercise running in a wheel; the new idea was to get them chasing their owner around in a virtual game.

How does it work? The team built an enclosed playspace adjoining the hamster's cage. In the game, the hamster, who likes running into tunnels, is encouraged to chase after a doll. On the player's computer, through which they can access the game from anywhere in the world, the doll appears as them. Adrian and his team are working on myriad other intriguing devices to enable subtle and uplifting communications between people – or in this case, between species, which explains the Greco-Latin game title: Metazoa Ludens – species at play.

Another great-but-unusual game is xBlocks, a playable art piece inspired by computer games. Looking like an Escher-inspired tabletop sculpture, its maze-like configuration of connected beams serves as the surface for a chase game

Metazoa Ludens: Would you like to play chase with a hamster?

xBlocks: Where physical and virtual play affect each other.

Fancy playing a computer game that's escaped from the screen?

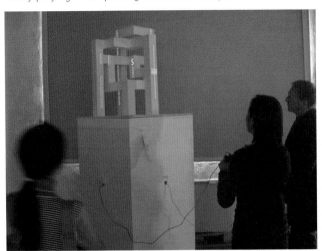

played using controllers. Tristam Sparks explained 'I was interested in the aspect of how a computer game might cross over into real space and affect traditional play. It turns the passive relationship between player and screen on its head', he explained. 'Hunting down your character and moving around the gamespace becomes very much a part of the experience'. Tristam created the work with colleague Victor Szilagyi.

In my survey, Tom, 36, asked for 'a really good railway-engineering type game', which it's hard to believe doesn't already exist. But here's what they've got to offer you, Tom, at Graz University of Technology: a train that isn't really there!

Invisible Train is a game you play using personal digital assistants (PDAs) to control virtual trains on a real wooden train track. The magic of the system is that

Invisible Train: This intuitive game shows the power of virtual reality.

the PDAs gauge exactly where they're looking in relation to the track, so that they can show the track, plus a virtual train running around it (it's as if the PDA screens were see-through). You can make the trains miss each other or crash, which players of the game have enjoyed: 'people understand how to use these applications often without introductions from our side. We noticed young children playing our games, exploring the game rules and how to operate the device on their own', researcher Daniel Wagner told me. The aim of the game is to demonstrate the power of this kind of 'virtual reality'.

Gamers Like Existing Games

Publishers take note: Gamers do enjoy the games they're already playing. Several of the survey respondents suggested that their favourite game would become absolutely perfect with the addition of one more vital ingredient. One 16-year-old gamer wanted a Grand Theft Auto Massively Multiplayer Role-Playing Game. Greg quite fancied Rise of Nations, but with driving. An 18-year-old female gamer put the icing on the cake with her suggestion of a role-playing game that also involved quests, and romance thrown in.

Lots of people wanted more games that exercised their cognitive faculties, emphasizing again the power of the medium to keep us thinking and extending our learning in a uniquely painless way. Cathie asked for something 'that had a point of view, taught me something and yet was compelling'. Catherine liked puzzle games and games to engage learners without them realizing. Sven requested a game that was 'intellectually and emotionally challenging, not only about dodging as many bullets as possible'. David, 70, thought we would benefit from a game 'that encourages good character and behaviour'.

And there's no need to think that we have to give up on the sheer pleasure of gaming at any stage. 'You're told you can't play computer games after a certain age', observes game-writer Aleks Krotoski. She thinks we're led to believe that play is a complete, childish waste of time. 'But, the more fun people have, the more they enjoy life and the more they'll contribute'.

Games Aren't Yet the Diverse Cultural Force They Could Be

But many games take too long to play, a problem that games of all kinds need to tackle if games are to attract an important target market. 'As a family man, I can't be involved in games that take hours upon hours to play any more', says Marko, 29. 'My ideal games have shifted towards multiplayer games that are designed for small groups of players. Ideally, a game would be playable without investing hundreds of hours into it, and it would foster a warm atmosphere of competition among its players. Good communications would be important as well.'

Marko, you might be describing the gaming holy grail. Something quick to play, that nonetheless offers all the friendly challenge and banter of a seriously time-consuming experience. Everyone wants this. 'Among a lot of professional women that I know, time is so short', says games researcher Constance Steinkuehler. 'The idea of sitting down for three hours doing something without immediate salient benefit is not realistic. Most women do two things at once – if they're not breastfeeding while writing their papers, they're not going to get it all done'.

> ❝ **Most** women do **two things** at **once** – if they're not **breastfeeding while writing** their **papers,** they're **not going** to get it **all done** ❞

One respondent to my survey said 'I would love to see games that fuse narrative with interactivity, and deliver emotional "closure" in, say, the length of a TV episode.'

Constance also expresses her views of the current state of games. 'For women – a lot of games are crap – they're about armies and shooting. 90% of games are not what I consider provocative for a broad audience.' This seems to be a common concern. 'The content is limited', says Aleks Krotoski. 'We're not yet seeing higher forms of self-expression.'

Games certainly haven't yet reached the same cultural status as other forms of media. Industry pioneer David Braben can see parallels from the past. 'Even books were lambasted at one time – Dickens, when serialised, was compared to a cheap penny dreadful', he tells me. 'Cinema was criticised as pap entertainment for its first few decades. Now the games industry is in that phase'.

How come we don't see more creative games coming out of the industry? One former games programmer told me 'Where I worked, they had a system where people could submit ideas for games, so that the "best" could be chosen and prototyped. But given the huge cost of developing a game, very few ideas ever saw the light of day. Anything that wasn't a guaranteed hit was seen as too big a risk to take, so the games which were developed were not generally the most interesting ideas.'

'There's sometimes more innovation than you see', says games writer Margaret Robertson. 'It might look like another WWII war game but there may be something different, at a structural level, under the skin. That said, I don't think it's a hotbed of unstoppable innovation.' What should we do to encourage creativity? 'My instinct tends to be to avoid design by committee, and let people trust their instincts'.

One potential route for more engaging and sophisticated computer games is to increase their psychological depth. 'What fascinates me is to query the motivations of characters; to persuade players to see things differently', says David Braben. 'In film, as in real life, you question motives. You start to empathise: why's he a bad guy? That enriches a story enormously.' Braben believes the computer power is now here to create a gaming experience that will win over those who still think games are for kids. 'Our technology allows you to play the lead in a story that can unfold in many different directions. It's on a knife-edge.'

The new technologies we've seen in this chapter may yet open up what future games can be, generating new ideas and experiments that take us forward. And the range of people entering the industry may be changing too. 'Historically only the people who loved games at the age of 12 entered the industry,' says Aleks Krotoski, 'but now we're seeing all kinds of people come in, primarily to the storytelling and visuals side.' There's more crossover with television and film, and with people making social software. 'Games are an interesting template for people to use to express themselves.'

There's more **crossover** with **television** and film, and with **people** making **social software**. Games **are** an **interesting template** for **people** to use to **express themselves**

If we're looking at a creative mashup across media, how might games develop? There's no way to predict, when there are so many creative minds at work. Already, there's some level of crossover between games and film, art, the web and to some extent television, although it's in its infancy. But the potential is huge. In our final story of this book (Machinima Man), find out how film-makers have crossed over into games in an innovative and slightly anarchic way – and see if it gives you any ideas.

At Frontier Developments Ltd, David Braben is developing The Outsider, a game 'on a knife-edge' that can unfold in multiple directions.

Machinima Man

Yin-Chien Yeap describes the strange spectacle of movie-making in the virtual world There.

'I am standing near a traditional-looking stone castle, when suddenly, a crowd of footsoldiers clad in improbable blue jumpsuits comes swarming out of a gate. While the main pack sprints purposefully across the courtyard, a few members of the party appear to be confused, stopping around the gate and not running with the others. "And . . . CUT". Everybody's still – the director is walking over to the non-runners to find out why they haven't followed the others for this shot. Everybody goes back through the gate, preparing for another take.'

'It's the typical grind of movie-making. But what is surprising is that all this is happening while I sit at home in the UK. The actors in the scene are located in various states around America, some in Ohio, some in California. But "here" in the virtual world of There, they have gathered to make an animated movie together.'

This is the world of machinima – animated digital movies made in virtual and game worlds. They are 'acted' by avatars and all use standard games to run. One of the most famous pieces of machinima is Red vs Blue, recorded using the first-person sci-fi shooter Halo and chronicling the misadventures and musings of two teams of Halo soldiers as they suffer existential angst, permanently trapped in a game without end. By using digital spaces, the storyteller can access sophisticated environments and props which come as standard with the game software. From canyons to cities, from rockets to rayguns – the machinima maker can virtually shoot scenes which are otherwise available only to huge-budget real-world film-makers.

The director of today's production is Francis_7, renowned throughout the There universe as master machinima maker and all-round nice guy.

He told me: 'After college I found that my supply of actors sort of vanished. I had more time and money, but no willing cast to be in movies'. After discovering There, and its unique real-time lip-synched voice-chat, he realized it was a prime candidate for 'live' machinima recording. 'Movie-making in There is pretty much like herding cats, or directing a stage play with a paper bag over your head', says Francis_7, modestly. 'It's hard to coordinate schedules as there is no way of telling how long something will take.' His There-based company Miracle Pictures ('If it's a good picture ... it's a Miracle!') now has an impressive portfolio of animated movies and shorts.

The movies made by machinima range from spectacular to terrible – but what is significant is the emergent nature of the movement. It uses the game software in ways not intended by the original developers, putting the means of media production into the hands of the individual. The videos made by these guerilla movie-makers are done without the involvement of any studio, any broadcaster or any production company. And thanks to the Internet, they can also be distributed without having to depend on traditional channels. The audience that machinima can reach on the web is enormous. Could this creative crossover between media be a picture of things to come?

The **videos made** by **these guerilla movie-makers** are done **without** the involvement of **any studio**, **any** broadcaster or any **production** company

Index